Mrs. Wakeman
vs.
the Antichrist

Mrs. Wakeman vs. the Antichrist

And Other Strange-but-True Tales from American History

ROBERT DAMON SCHNECK

JEREMY P. TARCHER/PENGUIN
a member of Penguin Group (USA)
New York

JEREMY P. TARCHER/PENGUIN
Published by the Penguin Group
Penguin Group (USA) LLC
375 Hudson Street
New York, New York 10014

USA · Canada · UK · Ireland · Australia
New Zealand · India · South Africa · China

penguin.com
A Penguin Random House Company

Copyright © 2014 by Robert Damon Schneck
Penguin supports copyright. Copyright fuels creativity, encourages diverse voices, promotes free speech, and creates a vibrant culture. Thank you for buying an authorized edition of this book and for complying with copyright laws by not reproducing, scanning, or distributing any part of it in any form without permission. You are supporting writers and allowing Penguin to continue to publish books for every reader.

"Psychic in the White House," "Holy Geist," and "The Wee-Jee Fiends" originally appeared in *Fortean Times Magazine* in slightly different forms.

Most Tarcher/Penguin books are available at special quantity discounts for bulk purchase for sales promotions, premiums, fund-raising, and educational needs. Special books or book excerpts also can be created to fit specific needs. For details, write: Special.Markets@us.penguingroup.com.

Library of Congress Cataloging-in-Publication Data

Schneck, Robert Damon.
Mrs. Wakeman vs. the antichrist : and other strange-but-true tales from American history / Robert Damon Schneck.
p. cm.
Includes bibliographical references.
ISBN 978-1-585-42944-8
1. Parapsychology—United States. 2. Supernatural. 3. Occultism—United States. 4. Curiosities and wonders—United States. 5. United States—History—Miscellanea. I. Title.
BF1028.5.U6S35 2014 2014022799
001.94—dc23

Printed in the United States of America
1 3 5 7 9 10 8 6 4 2

Book design by Meighan Cavanaugh

CONTENTS

Mrs. Wakeman
vs.
the Antichrist

The Wee-Jee Fiends

From the *Oakland (CA) Tribune*, December 26, 1919:

> **Richmond Milliner Is Run Down by Speeding Motorist, Who Fails to Halt Car After Fatally Injuring the Victim.**
>
> No trace has been found of the machine that struck Miss Moro at San Pablo and Potrero avenues, just out of Richmond toward El Cerrito. She was found unconscious in the road, the speed of the machine indicated by the finding of her hat 60ft [18m] away, but no assistance had been rendered her by its occupants.
>
> She was taken to the Craven Hospital in Richmond, where her death from a fracture of the skull and internal injuries followed. Richmond and El Cerrito officials are

seeking the machine which caused her death but with almost no clews upon which to work.

Chief of police W. H. Wood was confident that the driver would be caught: "We have the testimony of an eye witness who saw the car run the girl down and flee," he told the *Oakland Tribune*. "We know where the car was going and we expect to seize the guilty person at any time." But his prediction proved wrong.

The hit-and-run driver was not found, and eighteen-year-old Jennie Moro's funeral was held on December 31, possibly the last of 1919's 3,808 traffic fatalities to be buried that year. "Each year it becomes more and more dangerous for a person to walk the streets," declared the Census Bureau, but if Stutz Bearcats and Model T Fords endangered American bodies there was another, more subtle danger threatening their minds, and it would twist the Moro's sorrow into madness.

The Mania Begins

Jennie Moro came from an Italian family that lived in what was then the small Bay Area town of El Cerrito, California. She was survived by her recently widowed mother, Mary, fifty-one, and a twenty-nine-year-old sister named Josephine. She had two small children and was married to Charles Soldavini, a plumber. They lived together in a two-story frame building on San Pablo Avenue, near the place where Jennie was killed, and from which the late Mr. Naggaro Moro had run his blacksmith and plumbing businesses.[1]

The family apparently had a Ouija board since 1918, though they seldom used it and had no faith in its communications. When Jennie died, however, the Moros began holding séances and consulting the board in a psychical search for the hit-and-run driver.

Josephine Soldavini approached town marshal Curtis Johnson, "with a jumble of numbers which she claimed that she had received in a dream" and believed that they formed the fatal car's registration number. When a corresponding number was not found in the automobile register, the séances continued. Mrs. Moro contacted the spirit of her late husband, Naggaro, who threatened to punish her daughter's killer, and the family was "gradually drawn into the belief that communication with the dead was being had through the board and through dreams."[2]

The "board" at the center of their efforts was patented as a "toy or game" in 1891, and a popular craze by 1920. Most players took a lighthearted approach to the results, using it to find missing objects or learn the future ("Tell me Ouija, that's a dear / Who'll be president next year?"), while others worried about its effect on the user's mental equilibrium.[3]

At the University of Michigan, Ouija boards were reportedly "replacing Bibles and prayer books," so that a local nerve specialist was treating female students for "extreme nervousness" brought about by "too close association with the Ouija board and too great belief in its wandering. They had become fascinated by its message and had come to place so much trust in them that they were in a serious condition when they were turned over to him." Men were also vulnerable, and a member of the staff warned that "[T]he ouija is becoming a serious menace to this country."[4]

Séance in the House of Mystery

On February 25, the *Richmond Independent* reported that, "Tony Bena, a neighbour, said that Mrs. Moro came to his house . . . and said she was going to save him and his family. She had wept on his arm at the time and he had tried to calm her. This is the first time he had noticed anything peculiar in the actions of his neighbors."

A few days later, a hole appeared in the Moro-Soldavini yard (or, perhaps, a block away from their house) that was about the size of a grave, and appeared to have dirt added or removed every day. This looked like the work of the spirits to Mrs. Moro, her family, and a growing circle of séance participants that came to include two nephews, Louis and Henry Ferrerio, and the Moro's neighbors: John (Giovanni) B. Bottini, forty-five; his thirty-six-year-old wife, Santina, and their daughters Rosa, age twelve, and fifteen-year-old Adeline.

The high school principal described Adeline as one of her

brightest girls and said that she had been perfectly normal "until this change came down on her." The teenager came to believe that she was clairvoyant, a trance medium, and possessed by the spirit of Jennie Moro, who "was completely in control of her body dictating every action."[5] The spirit of "Mrs. Thomas, a colored woman who had been dead for some years," was also said to have power over her.[6]

As the séances continued, the spirits wanted Adeline to have a comb decorated with "six stones of different hue." But Mrs. Bottini was unable to find one and bought her daughter a six-colored corset instead. This, and other odd requests, might have been part of the preparations being made for a grand "Passion Display" that was expected to take place at five P.M. on March 3, when "the evil in all of them would be cast out" through the influence of Jennie Moro's spirit. The mystery of the hole would be revealed soon after.[7]

Adeline dreamed that evil spirits were in her clothes, so those were burned along with some money and, possibly, the Ouija board itself.[8] Mr. Bottini also bought her an expensive new dress, and possibly a $150 diamond ring; the spirits apparently liked clothing and jewelry.

With the Passion Display drawing near, séances went on twenty-four hours a day. Rosa Bottini was unable to keep food down and needed to be revived several times with "holy water." Adeline said that Rosa's hair must be cut to save her life and it was, along with that of another child, and the clippings burned to dispel evil spirits. There were now five children in the house, as well as Mrs. Tony Bena, who was threatened with "bodily harm" if she tried to leave.[9]

Mrs. Bena had been there twelve hours when the Ouija board commanded the group to collect her daughter. Finding the Benas's door locked "the enthusiasts beat upon it with a hammer. Tony Bena, worried concerning his wife's absence drove the messengers away and decided to seek police aid in breaking up the séance."

El Cerrito did not have a police department in 1920, so town marshal A. W. MacKinnon was informed that the two families had drawn their curtains, barred the door and were "acting queerly."

At three P.M. on March 3, MacKinnon asked Chief Wood, from neighboring Richmond, for help. They met at the Moro-Soldavini house—dubbed "the House of Mystery" by journalists—along with six officers and two patrol cars.

The police were refused entry but did not have to force their way in. Perhaps Chief Wood met the family after Jennie's death, or knew that the Moros and Soldavinis were "highly spoken for by neighbors as law-abiding hard-working Italian people." Whatever the reason, Father J. J. Hennessy, a pastor of St. Joseph's Catholic Church in Berkeley, was sent for and persuaded the group to open the door and let officers enter the house. Adeline was "scantily clad" or wearing her new dress, the children were hungry, and the communicants "in a state of high nervous excitement and nearing exhaustion from lack of food and sleep." When the group realized they were being arrested, Mrs. Moro reportedly screamed, "My husband is here and he will kill you!" Whether or not the late Mr. Moro was present, a "lively tussle" ensued and the eight Ouija board enthusiasts taken to the county hospital at Martinez. Mrs. Bottini went into a trance and told officers "she had gone through the torment of the crucifixion, and then, being addressed by the Deity through her daughter, she had been brought back to Earth."

John Bottini was released and instructed to appear in Judge R. H. Latimer's courtroom the next day, so the County Lunacy Commission could evaluate those who had been arrested. In the meantime, Bottini looked after his youngest daughters, while Mrs. Moro's cousin, Joe Ferrerio, cared for the Soldavini children.

The hearing lasted several hours. Tony Bena and Joe Ferrerio were present, and Rosa Bottini gave the panel of three doctors "a clear and lucid description of what took place." This contrasted with the account given by the four female "Ouijamaniacs" who talked "wildly" whenever the board was mentioned. All four were judged insane "on their own testimony," and Judge Latimer committed Adeline and Mrs. Moro to the state mental hospital at Stockton, and Mrs. Bottini and Josephine Soldavini to the Napa asylum. The men were released after they "disavowed their belief in the alleged messages of the board and said they took part in the séances in an effort to dissipate the hallucinations of the women."

Charles Soldavini reportedly burned the board that night,

but the Ouija's resilience is legendary and it continued to fascinate those living around San Francisco Bay.[10]

Ouijaphobia

Four days before the families were arrested, a brick was thrown through a jeweler's window, reportedly at a "suggestion from the Ouija board."[11]

A few days after that, Captain O'Day, of San Francisco's Potrero police station, filed a report with his chief on March 4 expressing concerns about officer Elmer H. Dean, who "had been acting peculiarly and talked much of the information he had obtained from a Ouija board. He said he had a message instructing him to capture some mysterious enemy." Dean borrowed a revolver from the station and did not report to work the next morning.

He was found at Berkeley and sent to the Anderson sanitarium at Fruitvale but escaped, jumping onto the running board of a passing car, pointing the gun at the driver, and demanding to be taken back to Berkeley. He undressed along the way (no small trick while clinging to the outside of a moving car) and when they reached downtown Oakland, the naked Dean took refuge in the Central Bank Building. A patrolman brought a blanket and returned him to the hospital, where doctors attempted to evaluate "the effect the

Ouija board produced upon his mind."[12] Such incidents were not restricted to California.

The citizens of Macon, Missouri, become so preoccupied with the board that "one person in five of the entire population . . . had fallen a wild-eyed victim to the strange malady" and preparations were under way at a local institution for their "wholesale reception."[13]

Back at El Cerrito, it was reported that "Ouija mania has gripped the entire city." A meeting held at town hall on March 4 resolved to ban the board and have the town's 1,200 residents examined to see if they were under its influence. A committee was formed to approach psychiatrists at the University of California and enlist their help.[14]

Meanwhile, the "varnished and nimble 'wee-gee,'" was being denounced from the pulpit ("People who consult the Ouija board rather than Christ are displaying a yellow streak"), in the lecture hall ("as dangerous as a shot-gun in the hands of a maniac"), and by newspaper editors ("time for an end to the tolerance that has given the Ouija a wide and claptrap popularity"). San Francisco's Spiritualist churches proposed a "Ouija board test" for the police force, claiming that "insanity of the kind disclosed by the Ouija board prevails to a degree 250 times greater among policemen than another other people."[15]

The board was called a drug "that is put into the brain directly . . . and the damage is swiftly and directly done," and an illness with a recognizable course. "Dementia Ouija usually does not manifest itself in the form of frank delusions or hallucinations, but rather in an insidious way. The victim first regards the instrument with amusement, later with interest, still later with mystification and finally when the mind is sufficiently debased by the insane business, with actual reverence."[16] Furthermore, Ouija madness was a communicable disease.

Sacramento's health department ordered detectives to break up Ouija board meetings, and that city, along with Oakland and Richmond, considered ordinances to prevent sales of the board. State senator William R. Sharkey prepared a bill to prohibit the "spirit's switchboard" in California altogether, but unlike the Prohibition of alcohol that began two months earlier, attempts to ban the board proved unsuccessful

Richmond discovered that it did not have the authority to prohibit Ouija boards, the citizens of El Cerrito were not subjected to mass analysis, and there is nothing to suggest that police "séance squads" carried out raids. In July, Oakland detectives *did* arrest a medium for producing "spirits" that advised her clients to buy oil stocks that she controlled, but this was not the "War on clairvoyants, spiritualists, séances and Ouija board manipulators" described by the press.[17] In fact, a determined anti-Ouija movement never appeared, and most of those deranged by the board soon recovered.

The fate of the naked policeman is not known, but the

four women at the center of the Ouija hysteria were freed before the end of April; their descendants still live at El Cerrito, where the events of 1920 are largely forgotten. The House of Mystery is also gone, and a Target superstore stands on the site.

Cinema de Ouija

Cerritoans might have put the business behind them, yet the story remains intriguing

In 2003, writer-director Ryan McKinney began work on a supernatural horror movie about a young married couple who move into a Victorian house where they discover Mrs. Moro's twice-burned Ouija board in the attic. The husband warns his wife not to touch it, but the film's promotional tagline is "One little question won't KILL me!"

McKinney "looked into some of the stories of what happened, what was reported, and then took it a level further to see what happened to people who participated in it."[18] The result was *The Invited*, starring Carlos Alazraqui and Pam Grier, which was released in 2010.

Films sometimes revive interest in the events that inspired them, and much of what happened in 1920 remains unexplained. What was the group trying to accomplish? Did Mary Moro, or the others, consider themselves psychic before the séances began? And why were the men released when John

Bottini is quoted as saying: "We believe in the Ouija board and our faith is unshaken. The board will drive away evil spirits. Do you think we look like maniacs?"[19]

In addition to insanity, Ouija boards have also been blamed for a handful of murders, but millions of divorces and suicides. But millions have experienced nothing more traumatic than a giggle. Nevertheless, it is worth remembering El Cerrito before dimming the lights, resting your fingertips on the planchette, and asking: "Is anybody there?"

Mrs. Wakeman vs. the Antichrist

On the morning of Monday, December 24, 1855, a man's bloody corpse lay on the floor of a house at New Haven, Connecticut. In life, he belonged to a small religious sect that believed he was possessed by the Antichrist, a belief that he more or less shared. As a result, he participated in his own death, during which he was bound and beaten with a stick, had his neck cut open, and was stabbed, to prevent the spirit's malignant power from harming their leader, Mrs. Wakeman. She was one of the more eccentric products of the Second Great Awakening, a religious revival that kept America at a rolling boil for nearly a century.

The First Great Awakening lasted from the 1730s to the 1770s, and during that time evangelizing ministers preached a passionate fire-and-brimstone religion that led to the growth of all denominations, particularly the Baptists and

Methodists. Around 1790, the Second Great Awakening began and forever changed the country's religious landscape.

Revivals, camp meetings, and circuit-riding preachers attracted church members in unprecedented numbers, especially in the South and West. It was also during this period that a pious farmer named William Miller calculated that Jesus would return to Earth around 1843. His prediction led to the most popular and sustained expectation of Judgment Day in American history, with stories, mostly untrue, told about Millerites dressed in "ascension robes" gathering on roofs, hilltops, and cemeteries, singing hymns, and waiting to rise into the sky.

When nothing happened, Miller revised his calculations and when these proved wrong, he stopped making predictions. Another preacher named Snow, however, claimed that the world would end on October 22, 1844; when it did not, the day became known as "the Great Disappointment." While most Millerites went on to join conventional churches or start new ones, millennial expectations were not confined to whites. The northern Paiute prophet, Wovoka, taught that the Ghost Dance ritual would reunite the Indians with their ancestors, while a "Messiah craze" swept black residents of Georgia in 1889, with no less than five Christs proclaiming that the Judgment was near, and causing a labor shortage.[1] America, however, has a long history of sects and cults.

Some, like the Seventh-Day Adventists and the Church of

Jesus Christ of Latter-day Saints, became part of the religious mainstream, but most were obscure or short-lived.

In Vermont, the Dorrilites were sexually promiscuous vegetarians who wore wooden shoes and sang songs "that would defile a brothel."[2] By 1800, their leader, William Dorril, was claiming to be invulnerable and while preaching that "No arm can hurt my flesh," a man stood up, punched Dorril in the face, and kept punching him until he admitted that it hurt; they disbanded soon after. Eighty years later, the spirit of Jesus entered red-haired George Jacob Schweinfurth and he set up a "heaven" at Rockford, Illinois, where several female disciples "conceived by the Holy Ghost" and had redheaded babies (Schweinfurth later joined Christian Science and became a life insurance salesman).[3] The alchemist and messiah Dr. Cyrus Reed Teed taught a "cellular cosmogony" in which the universe is a bubble of space within an infinite expanse of stone; Earth's surface is on the interior wall of the bubble, which surrounds and encloses the sun and sky. His followers ("Koreshans") carried out elaborate experiments to prove that the world is concave and built a utopian community called New Jerusalem at what is now Estero, Florida (when Teed died and failed to resurrect, his followers put him in a tomb that was swept away by a hurricane). While the Koreshans were merely eccentric, zealotry made groups like the Cobbites dangerous.

Preacher Cobb's first name is forgotten, but he arrived at White County, Arkansas, in 1876. One source claims he practiced "infant sacrifice," and while that is unlikely, the Cobbites did hold possessions in common, reportedly believed the sun rose and set at Cobb's command,[4] and demonstrated their faith by walking along roof ridges with their eyes closed. This might have gone on indefinitely, and produced nothing worse than an occasional broken neck, had local developments not put the group under pressure.

They were not popular in the neighborhood. Agitating against saloons made the Cobbites enemies, and Preacher Cobb interpreted the arrival of a drought as punishment for man's sins and a warning that the world might be coming to an end. With that, his followers at Gum Springs, Arkansas, destroyed their property and began dragging passersby inside to hear the gospel, whether they wanted to or not. Two men from the town of Searcy came to see what was happening and one of them, a bartender, apparently planned to amuse himself at the believers' expense.

When the pair arrived, the bartender reportedly made a sarcastic remark that infuriated the already overwrought Cobbites, who dragged him to an exposed tree root normally used as a chopping block and cut off his head with a dull axe. The gory trophy was kicked like a ball and a "ritual dance" performed around it, before being impaled on "a front yard picket for all to see."[5] The victim's companion escaped back to Searcy and returned with armed vigilantes.

Believing that faith made them invulnerable to weapons in the hands of the wicked, the Cobbites were defiant. Two were shot dead, most of the others ran away, and those who were captured were put on trial and released. Preacher Cobb reportedly fled into the woods or was escorted from the area by a posse, and nothing more is heard of him. (There is a postscript to the story; according to Heber Taylor of the White County Historical Society, the house where the murder took place "was used as a community amusement center for a while after the Cobbites left. That arrangement didn't seem to work too well. Some folks said the forms of the men killed there appeared and joined in the dances to the wail of the fiddle.")[6]

Though the bartender's death was gruesome, it happened far from the media and received little attention outside the state. In the Connecticut murder, "[a] bloody tragedy of this sort, enacted under the very eaves, as it were, of Yale College, in the intelligent, enlightened and pious city of New Haven, must strike every one who hears it with a sudden and creeping horror."[7] And there were newspapers at New Haven and New York City to make sure everyone heard about it.

What happened on the day before Christmas 1855 was the culmination of a long struggle between a woman named Rhoda Wakeman and the Antichrist. She was God's Messenger, whose divine mission left three dead and made *Wakemanite* synonymous with religious fanaticism for decades.

Married to Sin

Prophesying is a difficult trade. Jonah was swallowed, then vomited up, by a fish; Tiresias's gender was changed twice; and no one believed Cassandra. St. Stephen asked, "Which of the prophets have not your fathers persecuted?" before he was stoned to death,[8] and the children of Bethel mocked Elisha's baldness, saying "Go up, thou baldhead, go up thou baldhead!" God sent "two she-bears out of the wood, and tare forty and two children of them," but God did not send "she-bears" often enough to deter most critics, and Rhoda Wakeman's career, like those of her predecessors, was punctuated by difficulties.[9]

She was born Rhoda Sly on November 6, 1786, in Fairfield, Connecticut, the first of four children fathered by Phineas Sly and his unnamed wife. Sly later married Eunice Baker, who was fifty-three years old when she gave birth to Rhoda's half brother Samuel in 1803. At age four Samuel, called "Sammy," suffered a serious head injury that damaged his brain and left him weak-minded.

Around 1800, Rhoda married a distiller named Ira Wakeman (b. 1777) at Fairfield; they had fifteen to seventeen children, of which she acknowledged nine (the *Wakeman Genealogy (1630–1899)* mentions seven).[10] Little can be said about Mrs. Wakeman's spiritual development, though she reportedly attended Methodist meetings and read the Bible, Milton's *Paradise Lost*, and a popular devotional book titled

The Saints Everlasting Rest by the Rev. Richard Baxter, a "Treatise of the Blessed State of the Saints in their Enjoyment of God in Glory." In 1825, Ira threatened to kill her, and the prospect of meeting God unprepared provoked some kind of crisis in Mrs. Wakeman, who prayed until Jesus appeared.

He showed her the sufferings of the saints and martyrs and said, "Thou art justified forever—peace to thy soul!" This marked the beginning of "seven years of travail," when she believed Mr. Wakeman might murder her at any time; according to their daughter Selina, her mother's fears were well founded, for Mr. Wakeman "used to drink a great deal of liquor and frightened her a great deal because she was determined to get religion. I have heard him threaten her life, saying that if she spoke a word or read a word in the Bible he would be the death of her instantly. . . . I have known my father to carry a razor to bed with him threatening to kill her with it." His treatment left Rhoda Wakeman "partially deranged."[11] She produced a written account of her experiences and describes how he finally made up his mind to kill her, so "the enchantment of hell would then be broken and the world would be at peace. He told me that the world would never be at peace as long as God let me live."[12]

On the day of the murder, Wakeman declared, "Last Saturday night I took my razor and went before the glass to kill myself. I made a league with the devil, more steadfast and strange than ever, if he would clear me. And then I would Kill you first—and by the great Jehovah Christ I will do it—and they may execute me on the gallows." He lit a small fire, put two chairs in front of it, and told Mrs. Wakeman to prepare for death. She commended her baby to God, prayed, and sat in one chair while her husband sat in the other. He used "dreadful language and cursed God and d_____d me to hell. I thought when he stopped swearing he would cut my throat." Instead of a razor, though, Wakeman "drew a light on me from the fire," a length of burning wood, which he thrust into her heart, and it was "the last I knew of this world."[13]

She found herself surrounded by a thousand little black spirits that were preparing to take her away when a white spirit came down and the imps vanished. The white spirit escorted Mrs. Wakeman thousands of miles away, to a place of bright white clouds, where she had a series of visions:

> I went up to Heaven: there was a red light and many white clouds there: Christ came to me when I was in Heaven with his nails in his hands, spoke peace to my soul; because he spoke peace to my soul I raised up, and another spirit came to me and spoke saying, "Make your peace with God." I then kept on praying; he soon took me to Paradise and told me all about Adam and Eve and all the other spirits; this light then come on me so that I had to look up, and the spirits said I was numbered as one of them; I was taken up to Heaven from this place of light, and then saw Christ

> and all the Holy Angels; Christ had on the thorns and looked as he was when crucified; then saw God sitting upon his throne in all his glory; about the throne where all the angels in their white robes, and they were all happy spirits there; this spirit then came and took me back to earth, and when I got to earth again I saw my dead body lying on the floor; felt bad because I had come back to this wicked world again: I soon saw my wicked husband, who said, "By God, she's raised!" soon after I saw two [angels] came and spoke to me kindly and then Christ appeared to me and I fell down before him. And oh! How happy I felt! And how happy I then was![14]

The room was also filled with angels six inches tall and her husband repeated three times, "By God, she's raised!"

According to other sources, Ira Wakeman gave his wife a brutal beating that left her unconscious; nevertheless, she had an experience that she understood as a revelation. Some idea of the beliefs it inspired can be cobbled together from court testimony, newspaper interviews, and personal writings.

The Wakemanite Doctrines

Wakeman's faith can be summed up in twelve points. Three are unremarkable:

- A belief in the genuineness of the Bible.
- A belief in a God as a Supreme Ruler.
- That Jesus Christ came into the world to save it from sin.

The rest are specifically Wakemanite:

- That it is not legal to marry, and that all marriages are the consequence of worldly lusts.
- That she [Rhoda Wakeman] is a messenger sent by God to redeem the whole world from sin, and build up Christ's kingdom on Earth.
- That the devil has the power over death, and whenever his satanic majesty chooses, any sinner must die. She put great emphasis on the passage from Hebrews 2:14 (KJV), "Forasmuch then as children are partakers of flesh and blood, he also himself likewise took part of the same; that through death he might destroy *him that hath the power of death, that is the devil*" [my italics].
- That the curse was put on the world by the evil spirit, but that God will take it off for Christ's sake.
- That she has the power to destroy the world at pleasure, or bring the millennium whenever she wishes to do so.
- That God has invested her with supreme power, and that she can exercise this power on Earth.

- That she has the power to forgive sins.
- That she knows the thoughts of people by looking at their eyes.
- That the devil puts the evil spirit upon everybody who does not believe her doctrines.[15]

One of her most important beliefs comes from II Thessalonians 2:3–10, in the Apostle Paul's warning to his followers:

> 3 Let no man deceive you by any means: for that day shall not come, except there come a falling away first, and that *man of sin* be revealed, the son of perdition;
>
> 4 Who opposeth and exalteth himself above all that is called God, or that is worshipped; so that he as God sitteth in the temple of God, shewing himself that he is God. [KJV; my italics]

From these passages, Mrs. Wakeman came to believe that the "Man of Sin," or Antichrist, is an evil spirit that moves from one person to another in order to slay her and, by killing her, damn humanity and destroy the universe. Her husband was revealed as the Antichrist, and his unsuccessful attempt at murdering the prophetess demonstrated Mrs. Wakeman's immunity to earthly dangers such as a burning stick of wood thrust into the heart. (Had she been Roman Catholic, this incident might have been considered in terms of the "mystical piercing" or transverberation, described by saints like

Teresa of Avila, who was stabbed by an angel with a fiery arrow.) Mrs. Wakeman left home to live with a daughter and began her ministry by preaching from door to door.

When the prophetess next visited her husband, she had several devotees with her who tied him up. Mrs. Wakeman then "drew a knife or poniard, and with it made a most unnatural assault upon him, inflicting wounds of a very serious nature. The assault would doubtless then have proved fatal had it not been for the fear of some of her more responsible disciples, who becoming alarmed, put an end to the attack."[16] The wounds reportedly hastened Ira Wakeman's death at Fairfield on March 8, 1833.

Samuel Sly said that "he was not killed by any of us, he came to his end when he was fifty years of age by the termination of his league with the Devil. I understood from the revelation given to my sister that his league with Satan was that he should live in health and comfort for fifty years, and during that time he was to work the deeds of wickedness."[17] (That means Ira made a pact with the devil at age six.) In addition to trying to kill God's Messenger, he bewitched all the invalids in the area and she saw "streams of fire fly out of the eyes of her husband and had seen little devils about two feet high dance around him in the room."[18]

Wakeman's death, however, did not put the prophetess beyond the reach of the Man of Sin.

Samuel's Conversion

Little is known about Samuel Sly's and Mrs. Wakeman's activities from 1833 to 1840. On July 3, 1836, however, two of her future disciples, Justus Washington Matthews and Mehitable Sanford were married; also that year, at Worcester, Massachusetts, the "prim and precise" Thankful S. Hersey was teaching children to read at her infant school. In 1842, when Millerism was at its height, she closed the school, "much to the regret of parents in that part of the town," to prepare for Christ's return.[19] At some point after the Great Disappointment she came into contact with Mrs. Wakeman and became a passionate disciple.

In 1840, Sly was living at Orange in New Haven County with an unnamed female between fifty and sixty years old—presumably Mrs. Wakeman—and a year later they were at Greenfield. There she did "all that lay in her power to promote the good of those around her," and converted Samuel.[20]

He sometimes attended Methodist meetings, but one Sunday Mrs. Wakeman offered to explain her views of the Bible and an "unseen power" convinced him to remain. She read passages from Hebrews 2:14 (KJV), which refers to "him that hath the power of death, that is the devil," the power that had been Ira Wakeman's but now belonged to the second Man of Sin, Eben Gould.

Sly accepted everything Rhoda Wakeman said and stated

that the "foundation of our faith" is "that the devil has the power of death, which I had thought before was a power of God . . ."[21] (Why Mrs. Wakeman thought Gould was the Antichrist, and even his identity, are unclear. Her daughter, Sarah, was married to an Alden Gould, and the census of 1840 lists an Eben Gould living in Fairfield, Connecticut, who was between fifty and sixty years old; was he Alden's father?) Samuel embraced the creed with enthusiasm, preaching to anyone who would listen and kneeling to pray anywhere.

When he asked permission to pray at Mrs. Mary Ann Wharton's house, she agreed but added, "'pray short, Sammy,' for he was very tedious—he would pray all day."[22] Sly was considered a "very good, harmless, prayerful man," though he "acted and spoke like a child" and was always poor. He often worked as a farmhand but would neither slaughter livestock nor step on a beetle, and he seems to have been regarded with the kind of good-humored exasperation reserved for children and harmless eccentrics. ("Once when he called at my house to get a chicken, and wanted me to kill it because he was afraid to do so, but I did not. Some time after, I saw the chicken in his yard and asked him why he had not killed it, and he said he would not do so for all the world."[23])

After Sly's conversion he stopped walking past the houses of people with the "power," and upon learning that Mary Ann Wharton was a "great enchanter," he would run across the street to avoid meeting her. (It might be reading too much into a statement nearly 150 years old, but the situation seemed to amuse Mrs. Wharton.) In addition to enchanters, Sly believed the neighbors were conspiring to kill him and set out across Connecticut to escape them and preach Mrs. Wakeman's gospel.

He met some Mormons and tried converting them while they tried converting him, endured what he considered persecution, and sold items that his half sister wove on a loom (she "tried by excessive work at a loom to support herself").[24] After work on Sundays, Sammy rode many miles for the "privilege of seeing her, and of hearing her expound the prophecies and tell of the revelations to her, guiding us in our career, was a good reward."[25]

The Mad Prophetess

Newspaper illustrations were rare in the 1850s, and no description of Samuel Sly or Mrs. Wakeman has turned up beyond a journalist calling her "the very personification of the wonderful women that lived in Salem in the sixteenth [*sic*] century."[26]

Salem, Massachusetts, is synonymous with witches, yet the Nutmeg State has some claim to being the most hag-ridden place in New England. Connecticut executed its first witch in 1647, put the last one on trial fifty years later, and hanged ten more in between. Mrs. Wakeman certainly believed in all the appurtenances of *maleficia*, including demonic pacts and magical poisons, yet she always used the word *enchanter* and, despite looking the part, was not a witch but a lunatic.

She struck some as a "naturally pretty clever sort of woman" and, though her beliefs were often absurd, no one doubted the sincerity with which she held them.[27] Mrs. Wakeman's daughter, Caroline Lane, considered her illuminated by "light from heaven" and accepted her teachings, while agreeing with her sister Selina that Ira Wakeman's cruelty left their mother unhinged.

The prophetess's behavior was certainly odd. She wept at the sight of people walking to churches that believed God had the power of death and not the devil ("she could find it in the Bible"), spirits appeared to Mrs. Wakeman at night begging her to preach, and Caroline often found her mother sobbing at two or three in the morning.[28] Evil enchanters were everywhere, and many of her relationships followed a distinct pattern.

She apparently held people in the highest regard until they said or did something critical of the prophetess; doing that exposed them as wizards, possessed by an evil spirit, or it meant they were the Antichrist. Moreover, the better her opinion, the further they fell; "Hurld" like Lucifer "headlong flaming from the Ethereal Skie / With hideous ruine and combustion down/to bottomless perdition . . ." (Theology aside, *Paradise Lost* probably appealed to Mrs. Wakeman's sense of drama). The experience of Ephraim Lane, Caroline's husband, is typical.

According to Ephraim, "There was nobody like me with Mrs. Wakeman," until 1852, when he said, "'Mother, there's nothing in your doctrines—it's all a delusion.'" With that, she became afraid of Ephraim and decided that he had "a bad spirit that wanted to kill the good spirit in her."[29] (What "having a bad spirit" meant is unclear. It might refer to Leviticus 20:27 [KJV], "A man also or a woman that hath *a familiar spirit*, or that is a wizard, shall surely be put to death . . ." [my italics]). Caroline's turn came on March 31, 1854, when the Wakemanites were excommunicating Charles Willoughby, who was another one of Mrs. Wakeman's sons-in-law. They accused him of causing all the storms that winter and covering Sammy with a thousand little devils that crawled over his head and back, but Caroline expressed doubts and that frightened Mrs. Wakeman, who said, "'Don't call me Mother—anybody that wants to kill me needn't call me Mother.'"[30] This reaction might explain why her closest associates included Thankful Hersey, described as Mrs. Wakeman's "echo," and a brain-damaged half brother who made her paranoia his own.

In time, Sammy collected enough money to free Mrs. Wakeman from the "hard bondage of weaving," and moved into a series of rented houses at New Haven where they were able to hold regular meetings.[31]

City of Scholars and Guns

New Haven is an old city by American standards. Founded by Puritans in 1638, it has the full complement of stories appropriate to New England's ancient settlements, including a phantom ship that sailed into the harbor sometime in the 1640s, broke apart, and vanished in a "smoky cloud." The Rev. Cotton Mather told the story in his *Magnalia Christi Americana* (1702), and Longfellow published a poem about it in 1858:

And the masts, with all their rigging,
Fell slowly, one by one,
And the hulk dilated and vanished,
As a sea-mist in the sun![32]

The city is best known, however, for Yale University, which was established in 1701 to educate the Puritan theocracy, as well as Broadway previews and firearms. Eli Whitney opened a rifle factory there at the end of the eighteenth century, and by the middle of the nineteenth, so much weaponry was produced at New Haven that it was called "the Arsenal of America." Mrs. Wakeman's preaching attracted workers and farmers from the surrounding areas.

They met every Sunday and once again during the week. Sammy described their worship as "prayer and singing by the faithful believers, and then my sister would select quotations from the Bible, and explain them, and then the spirit of the Almighty would descend on her, and she would reveal to us the sayings of the Deity, and guide us in our temporal as well as spiritual doings."[33] There were also two important developments in 1845.

First, Mehitable Matthews's nephew, Charles Sanford, was released from the Hartford Retreat for the Insane. He began attending their services, and numerous prayer meetings were held on Sanford's account, presumably to cure his insanity.[34] In addition, a seventeen-year-old named Amos Hunt joined the group.

In 1850, Mrs. Wakeman and Samuel were living in a small house on Ashmun Street by the wall of the Grove Street Cemetery, almost under the eaves of Yale. They supported themselves in various ways: boarding children and selling fruits, berries, and "decoctions of syrups and herbal medicines" that Mrs. Wakeman distilled from plants gathered by Sammy.[35] These proved popular, and the widow acquired a reputation as a healer or quack doctor whose clients reportedly included an old farmer from Woodbridge named Sperry; he played an unfortunate role in Wakemanite history. Caroline persuaded her mother to charge something for the remedies, but the prophetess "was not sent for money" and gave away most of what she earned.[36]

The Third Man of Sin

Over the next few years, the Wakemanites went quietly about their business while Amos Hunt came to hold an honored position among them.[37] Sammy described him as "a firm believer in our doctrines and for his deeds of goodness was looked upon as a mainstay of our body. He held continual meetings, and induced many to join us. We looked upon him as almost sanctified. . . ."[38] Demons, however, are notorious for harassing the devout; St. Jerome was troubled by phantom dancing girls, Martin Luther had to throw an ink pot at the devil, and Hunt used to visit Samuel's house "pretending to come that he might be relieved [of] the bad spirit. . . ."[39] He eventually fell and, when it happened, "his fall was the greater."[40]

According to Mrs. Wakeman, it happened after she and her followers met for regular Sabbath worship on November 29, 1855 (her recollection is faulty since November 29, 1855, was a Thursday). They apparently brought food to meetings, and Amos Hunt and his wife arrived with a pie wrapped in paper and seven cakes carried in a tin pail. Sammy put the food on the kitchen table and when they sat down to potluck dinner, Mrs. Wakeman ate a slice of pie and one and a half cakes, then became violently ill. She later described what happened, saying:

> I had a dreadful pain in my stomach and chest, and [whispering very confidentially as she leaned over her large Bible] I don't tell it often, but I puked. I was dreadful sick, and I put my thumb and finger in my mouth and pulled out something—, about so long [two or three inches], and then I puked again and pulled out another, and they was the sperits he put into the pizen to kill my sperit while the pizen killed my body.[41]

The prophetess claimed that her followers almost died from the poison—Samuel and a female Wakemanite reportedly felt sick—but she spent two days in agony before visiting Dr. E. C. Chamberlain, who was Mrs. Wakeman's doctor for six years and considered her insane. She began seeing Dr. Chamberlain when her other physician, Dr. Gray, turned out to be an enchanter.

Samuel reportedly took the uneaten food to Dr. Benjamin Silliman at Yale, a renowned chemist who apparently made himself available to the local eccentrics (a statue of him stands in front of the Sterling Chemistry Laboratory). According to Mrs. Wakeman, Silliman found enough poison in each cake to kill ten men, but before he identified it, the prophetess announced that the truth had been revealed to her.[42]

God's Messenger was immune to arsenic or other common substances that might sicken her followers, so food had to contain a magical poison made from the "brains of a man, the oil of men bones, the eyes of dogs, the eyes of roosters, garden basil, topaz stone, copper, zinc, platina [platinum] and the entrails of common toads."[43] It might have also been a simple case of *E. coli* (particularly if everyone got sick), but some believed that Hunt intentionally doctored Mrs. Wakeman's dinner to see if she was "human and not divine."[44]

After ten years of Wakemaniteism, the "bad spirit" troubling him might have been doubt. Perhaps he suspected that Mrs. Wakeman and her various claims, including invulnerability, were not genuine; if so, then Hunt discovered the truth and paid a price for it.

Eben Gould, the Man of Sin, had passed away, and "the power of death was scattered by Satan," but it was obvious who was "next to take the power."[45] Hunt made "a league with the devil" and to "him was given all the power that was ever on the earth for sin"; this might have sounded ludicrous to outsiders but not to Wakemanites.[46] When Sammy said that Hunt should be "given up as a living sacrifice to God," whose "death will bring the redemption in the twinkling of an eye," he was not speaking metaphorically, and Hunt offered them a cash settlement.[47] Despite Hunt's being an assassin, apostate, and Man of Sin, an arrangement was worked out so that Mrs. Wakeman's lawyer and former governor of Connecticut, the Hon. Henry Dutton, accepted $500 on her behalf.

As with the Cobbites before them, pressure was building on the Wakemanites. Beyond the continual threat of enchanters and evil spirits, Mrs. Wakeman was betrayed—almost murdered—by a trusted disciple and then accepted money from the Man of Sin. When Hunt sued to get it back, the prophetess declared that "should he gain his suit the world will irretrievably be destroyed and cast into the 'outer darkness,'" and though she would not touch the money, by taking it "an evil influence fell on us."[48]

They had compromised with the devil, and redemption would require something extraordinary, for "it is the blood that maketh an atonement for the soul."[49]

The Reluctant Antichrist

By December 1855, Rhoda Wakeman and Samuel Sly were living in a small house, a story and a half tall, at Beaver Street (or possibly in an alley between Beaver Street and Dixwell). There is no mention of children being boarded there—Amos Hunt had used magic to "take the good influence and innocence from them"—but the rooms were crowded with Wakemanites, and at some point the Man of Sin's spirit left Hunt and moved into Justus Washington Matthews.[50]

Unlike earlier Men of Sin, one of whom opposed Mrs. Wakeman's pretensions with violence, and another with poison, Matthews was an unremarkable thirty-seven-year-old who worked at a pistol factory. He attended meetings with his wife, Mehitable, and her sister, Polly Sanford, but was not an outstanding Wakemanite nor did he enjoy close contact with Mrs. Wakeman. There is no obvious reason why the evil spirit chose him, but its presence was revealed when Mehitable began experiencing convulsions; Mrs. Wakeman then fell sick, and in the hyper-vigilant atmosphere following the assassination attempt, that was apparently enough.

Matthews was cooperative. He did not object when "members of the sect first attempted to drive out the evil spirit by giving the poor man copious amounts of tea brewed from the bark of witch hazel trees."[51] (Unlike Rowan trees, which "put the witches to their speed," witch hazel is not a traditional apotropaic and belief in its power to drive off evil seems to have been one of Mrs. Wakeman's personal crotchets.[52] (The *witch* in *witch hazel* comes from the Old English *wican*, meaning "to bend." Flexibility made witch hazel branches popular with dowsers for use as dowsing rods.) Etymology aside, the tea did not work, and the Wakemanites likely prayed over Matthews and begged him to give up the evil spirit.

Around the twenty-first of the month he began a three-day fast while Sammy cut a long branch of witch hazel and put it in the cellar.

Knife, Fork, and Stick

On December 23 the Wakemanites began conducting Sabbath worship at two P.M. in an upstairs room of the house.

Mrs. Wakeman had about fifteen followers at the time, and since there was a full moon that night they were able to come and go until early Monday morning.[53] (If traditional beliefs about the full moon are true, its influence may have contributed to subsequent events.) Rhoda Wakeman, Samuel Sly, Thankful S. Hersey, Abigail Sables, and Julia Davis were already living at the house, while those attending services included Polly and Almeron Sanford, Israel Wooding, Betsy Keeler, farmers from Hamden, and Josiah Jackson, a gray-haired black man who worked as a porter at the train station; he was a familiar figure around New Haven and "moved within the group on a basis of complete social equality."[54] Jackson used a witch hazel walking stick given to him by Sammy "to keep enchantment away." (He later said, "Some persons think that colored people have a kind of conjuration power, but I got this idea [for the witch hazel stick] from *white folks*.")[55]

"It was generally understood that Matthews would be there that night, and it was expected that a special effort would be made to get the evil spirit out of him."[56] Sammy built a fire in the stove of the front room at around ten that evening and Justus Matthews arrived soon after. He sat down, removed his boots, and was warming his feet when the evil spirit began tormenting Mrs. Wakeman. The gaze of the Man of Sin was capable of causing harm, so Polly Sanford blindfolded her brother with a black silk handkerchief, "because silk would keep off his evil power."[57] She asked him if he was willing to be bound with a cord, and Matthews said he would "if it would bring the millennium, or subdue the evil power in him."[58] Polly Sanford then tied his wrists together behind his back, saying, "I do this for the Glory of God, and in the fear of the Lord."[59] When the exorcism began, Matthews was on a day bed; he later moved to a rocking chair and ended up on the floor.

For two hours, the Wakemanites alternated between the upper floor, where they prayed for the devil to be driven out of Matthews, and the front room, in order to badger and beg him to renounce the evil spirit. Josiah Jackson "told Matthews he was killing the old woman, and that I would not let him into my house sooner than I would a mad dog."[60] Almeron Sanford and Israel Wooding said that he was "drawing away her [Mrs. Wakeman's] spirit with his evil powers" as well as harming his own wife, and that it was better to have him die than to have Mrs. Wakeman and the whole world die.[61] There was a general agreement that it would be better if Matthews died, and he was reportedly willing, if it would "quench the evil spirit."[62]

The prophetess spent the night upstairs experiencing bizarre and excruciating torments. Around midnight "she was in great distress and could hardly breathe," then "[l]aid down to keep from fainting."[63] An hour later she claimed to be dying from creatures crawling around inside her; Josiah Jackson later testified, "She said she had three live creatures in her, which were crawling up her throat and choking her. Put my hand on her chest and stomach, and *I felt them*!" Sly,

Hersey, and Wooding rushed downstairs saying, "He's killing the messenger, he's killing the messenger!" And with a billion unredeemed souls poised to drop into hell, Samuel acted.[64]

Sly claimed that Matthews said, "You had better kill me," to which Sammy replied, "No Mr. Matthews, we will not do that," and went to retrieve the witch hazel branch, a piece of wood one inch in diameter and two and a half feet long, to "knock this evil spirit out of him."[65] As Matthews sat bound and blindfolded, Sly drew the curtains, secured the door by putting wooden wedges into the latches, and struck the helpless man a blow to the right temple, knocking him to the ground. He hit him several more times, then, feeling "urged on by some influence," cut Matthews's throat with a small pocketknife.[66] There was a fork in the room used for lifting the stove lid, and he plunged it into Matthews's chest twelve times (one source claims the punctures were done in the shape of a cross to release the evil spirit).[67] "Uncle Sammy," who was clearly not harmless, said of the murder, "The influence I was under led me to do this: I was influenced by a wrong spirit to go further than I had anticipated, or had any idea of."[68]

Matthews's brother-in-law, Almeron Sanford, heard a gurgling sound coming from the front room and pounded on the door, but the others held him back, saying, "If he's killing himself he'll be raised." There was another gurgling noise, the sound of blows, and cries of "Oh! Oh! Oh!" Unsure what to do next, some left for home or went back upstairs to pray. By two o'clock in the morning, Mrs. Wakeman felt well enough to notice strange noises coming from downstairs and told Betsey Keeler that "all was not right below."[69]

A half hour later Sammy opened the door. He went to the back room, where Thankful Hersey used a basin of water to wash the blood from his clothing. The shirtsleeves must have been too saturated to save, for they were torn off and burned, which suggests that cutting a throat with a two-inch blade is close and messy work. Sly's witch hazel stick, with Matthews's blood and hair still adhering to it, was dropped through the hole of the privy and the knife placed next to Matthews's body to make it look like he committed suicide. Sammy then wiped at the blood on the floor and went upstairs to pray while Matthews cooled and coagulated.

Josiah Jackson feared that the corpse could still harm the prophetess and told the Sanfords to remove it, but after a long night of worship and murder, the Wakemanites needed sleep. Polly Sanford stayed at Beaver Street, but Almeron walked home, returning at nine A.M. with nineteen-year-old Willard Matthews, the eldest of the dead man's five children, who was out looking for his father; Sanford seems to have brought his nephew there intentionally. (For a detailed account of the morning's comings and goings, see "Woodbridge and the Wakemanites a Hundred Years Ago," a paper read by Grace Pierpont Fuller at the annual meeting of the Woodbridge and Amity Historical Society in December 1955.)

Entering the silent house, Willard opened the door to the front room, where:

> the body lay upon the floor, with the head towards a bed in the room; and it was found with the face turned towards the window, lying upon the left side, and very nearly in the middle of the room. Clotted blood and hair lay upon the floor around him, and several pools of blood were found near his head. It was truly an awful scene to witness. The throat was cut nearly from ear to ear, and his head seemed to be nearly severed from his body.

The wound was so big it appeared to be inflicted with a hatchet, and

> [a] small rope was found on the floor, and marks of a rope were discovered on his wrists, and it was evident that the wrists had been bound by this rope.[70]

Willard exclaimed, "Oh! dear, father has killed himself."[71] After recovering from the initial shock, he went to the house of a neighbor, who summoned the justice of the peace. With that, the dream world Rhoda Wakeman created and shared with her followers began its fatal collision with the state of Connecticut.

Sheriff Leander Parmalee arrested everyone present the night before and convened a jury of inquest. They heard evidence on Christmas, and continued to sit until the twenty-sixth, when the postmortem was held and Sammy decided to confess. Holding a Bible and speaking in "fear of the Lord," he told the story to the jurors, who decided to release everyone except Sammy, Thankful Hersey, Josiah Jackson, Abigail Sables, and Mrs. Wakeman; they went back to jail to await the grand jury. Meanwhile, journalists were busy reporting the crime.

For the *New York Times* the murder was a "Horrible Case of Fanaticism" and one of the "Frightful Effects of Millerism," but Americans of the period called almost any violence or insanity motivated by religion "Millerism."[72] In fact, Mrs. Wakeman belonged to an earlier generation of mystics, one that included Joseph Smith Jr., founder of the Latter-day Saints movement, and the "Electrical Psychologist," the Rev. John Bovee Dods, who experienced phenomena similar to the Hydesville Rappings of 1848. Like Smith's *Book of Mormon* and Dods's lectures, Mrs. Wakeman preserved her revelations in writing; she was anxious to have them with her, so a reporter from the *New York Daily Tribune* agreed to visit Beaver Street in the company of Ephraim Lane and retrieve the "sacred papers."

Neighbors believed that the murder left the house haunted, but Matthews's bloody ghost did not rise to disturb the journalist as he climbed the stairs to Mrs. Wakeman's room. The papers, ten handwritten pages carefully bound with thread and protected by the inevitable witch hazel bark, were under the prophetess's bed in a square basket and rolled up in paper of a "singular color."

He returned to the New Haven County Jail where:

> The old hag Wakeman then advanced toward me, and, seizing my hand, clasped it in her bony fingers, and with a vacant stare in her eyes and fiendish grin upon her old wrinkled face, congratulated me upon my escape from this tormentor Lane. She said that she had it revealed to her from God that Lane was watching an opportunity to murder me, and she advised me to procure a witch hazel walking stick immediately, which would prevent him from murdering me, or even approaching me hereafter. She added that, "if I should ever shake hands with Lane the evil spirit would enter out of him and *into me*."[73]

For the reporter, it was obvious that Rhoda Wakeman was too old, ugly, and deluded to take seriously, yet she had a remarkable aptitude for getting others to kill. And the next two murders were bloodbaths.

The Mad Woodcutter

Charles Sanford was the unlikely offspring of a family whose name "is an honored one in Connecticut." As an anonymous note written in the margin of an 1856 article points out, though, "This sad case might have occurred in any family."[74]

At twenty-seven or twenty-eight years old, the oldest of Ruel and Sarah Sanford's seven children was a strange specimen. He had a protruding jaw that stuck out farther than his nose, limped heavily as a result of either a clubfoot or an accident, was chronically insane, and had an advanced case of tuberculosis. What bothered him the most, however, were cramps; Sanford suffered from muscular or abdominal cramps and believed they were being inflicted on him by magic. Whether he reached that conclusion himself or by attending Wakemanite meetings is unknown, but prolonged contact with the prophetess could not have improved Sanford's mental condition, and two years of relative sanity ended with the violent death of his uncle, Justus Matthews.

On Christmas Eve, Sanford caused a disturbance at the Hamden Plains church by telling the minister that he (the minister) "had said enough, and had better stop talking and let him [Sanford] talk."[75] Despite this outburst and a history of institutionalization, Sanford must not have seemed dangerous. Even when he came hobbling out of his parents' house with an ax on the morning of January 1, it was normal, for he was a woodcutter. Why he also carried a three-foot-long hickory club that was sharpened at both ends and covered in undecipherable writing is harder to explain.

The Sperry-Umberfield Massacre

The Sanfords lived at Hamden, two and a half miles from the Woodbridge home of Enoch Sperry. Mr. Sperry was known for his integrity in business, a natural genius for figures, and piety; he greeted the first day of 1856 with a prayer that "[m]ade allusion to the incoming of the new year, remarking that to God alone it pertained to guide its import to him and his. His entire prayer now seems to have been an almost inspired allusion to the sad catastrophe which has taken him from the bosom of his family."[76] That was not till later in the morning, though; in the meantime, a neighbor had borrowed the box of his sleigh and Mr. Sperry hitched a pair of sled runners to the farm horse and went to collect it.

At sixty-nine years old, his health was generally good despite occasional fits and a "stroke of palsy" that left his face partly paralyzed; Sperry reportedly visited Mrs. Wakeman for various complaints (according to Sammy, he "used to come to my sister to purchase of her syrups as she made to cure him of little aches").[77] He walked beside the animal down the snow-covered roads, keeping a handkerchief pressed against the paralyzed part of his face as protection from the cold. With hoofbeats muffled and the runners shushing along, it would have been very still: just jingling harness chains, crows cawing overhead, and an occasional snort from the horse. Grandma Moses painted rustic winter scenes like this but her pictures are peaceful and nostalgic and never include an ax-wielding homicidal maniac.

At around eleven A.M. Charles Sanford and Enoch Sperry met by a small brook on the way to Amity Road. Whether it was a chance encounter, or the woodcutter deliberately chose the isolated spot to lie in wait is unknown, but the men were acquainted and might have spoken before Sanford struck,

> first on the right temple with the head of the axe; then another blow just above the right ear, both of which produced fractures of the skull. He was then struck with the edge of the axe on his neck, the blow entering just under the chin, which it wounded and nearly severed the head from his body . . .[78]

Steam was still rising from the exposed stumps of Sperry's neck when Sanford left.

He tramped off through the woods while the phlegmatic horse continued on its way to Amity Road, where it entered the stable of the Clinton Hotel and halted. One of Mr. Sperry's neighbors, Samuel F. Perkins, recognized the horse passing by without a driver and, suspecting that the old man had a fit, resolved to check on him later that afternoon.

Sanford arrived at the farm of Ichabod Umberfield sometime between two and three o'clock. He entered the house, placed the ax and hickory club in the hall, and found the housekeeper, Lucy Deming, washing the kitchen floor. Slipping an arm around her waist, he invited Mrs. Deming into the hallway, whereupon she slapped him and he left the room.

Carrying his ax into another room, Sanford met ten-year-old Eliza A. Deming, who recognized him and fled. She took refuge in a bedroom with Mrs. Deming, who locked the door. Eliza opened a window and called to Mr. Umberfield outside, "Charles Sanford is in the house with an axe and he is crazy—you must come in."[79]

Umberfield was seventy-one and could have pretended not to hear her, but he went inside and found Sanford seated by the stove. Pulling up a chair, Umberfield tried engaging the young man in conversation, but got no reply; perhaps he was sulking over the housekeeper's rejection. After two minutes' silence, Sanford gathered his tools, stood up, and limped toward the door. This took him behind Umberfield's chair, where he paused to bring the ax down on the old man's head.

Umberfield dropped to the floor with his skull splintered, groaned, and was struck a second time. Mrs. Deming opened the door in time to see the third and final blow sink into her employer's neck, where it left just four inches of skin and the windpipe connecting them. Blood was pumping onto the floor and Eliza began screaming, which annoyed Sanford, who followed the fleeing child, saying, "Stop your noise or you'll get your head chopped off." He went outside to clean the ax in the snow and someone locked the door behind him, so Sanford headed back into the forest.[80]

There he met a black man named Philip Samson, who was busy chopping wood. "Mr. Samson was a tall and very large man. Charles went to work trimming out the wood but did not molest Samson. On being asked why he didn't kill Samson, he said 'he was too big for me.'"[81]

Hew and Cry

Samuel Perkins went to check on Mr. Sperry at three o'clock in the afternoon and found his mangled corpse lying in a ditch by the side of the road, still clutching a handkerchief. The body was carried to Sperry's home and two doctors were summoned to examine the remains; a messenger also left for New Haven to inform his sons, while neighbors began looking for the killer.

Following his trail through the snow was not difficult, and it must have been near dark when Officer Lucius Doolittle, with a posse of seven men armed with cudgels and farm tools, caught up with Sanford near the junction of Brooks and Downs Roads by the Umberfield house.[82]

Sanford, as might be expected, fought like a madman. He attacked them all at once and managed to land a glancing blow on Officer Doolittle's shoulder with the ax; a Mr. Peck, however, succeeded in pressing the tines of a pitchfork against Sanford's chest, and that gave a Mr. Gorham the opportunity to knock him down with a club. While the men escorted their battered captive to jail, Charles Sanford said he had been en route to slaughtering the remaining Umberfields.

Two inquests were held that day. The first, at six o'clock, heard no direct evidence against Sanford and therefore named some person or persons unknown as responsible for the death of Enoch Sperry. As for motive, "It is evident that Mr. Sperry was not murdered maliciously. For he was not known to have an enemy, and had been specifically kind to his assassin. Neither was there any intention of robbery, for a sum of money was found in his pockets when his body was discovered." This led to the conclusion that "the murder of Matthews excited Sanford to a desire to copy it. This is more likely, when it is considered that he struck the blows after a similar manner to those inflicted by Sly."[83] (According to one story, Sanford heard that his uncle was possessed and was on his way to kill him, but met Mr. Sperry first.)[84] The second inquest at nine o'clock found Charles Sanford responsible for the death of Ichabod Umberfield, but could not suggest a motive; from the woodcutter's perspective, however, it was self-defense, for "he had a cramp, and if he had not murdered Mr. Sperry and Mr. Umberfield, the cramp would have killed him."[85]

Dr. Pliny A. Jewett examined both bodies and found that the wounds resembled each other and could have been inflicted by Sanford's ax. He also tried, without success, to decipher the writing on the club, which was described as "in the style of much of the revelation documents in the 'unknown tongue;' it is therefore presumed to be some extracts from the 'Wakeman revelations.'"[86]

Judging by the number of surviving newspaper articles

devoted to the crimes, Justus Matthews's murder received far more coverage than those of Messrs. Sperry and Umberfield. If this impression is accurate, it is also unexpected when the latter involved two prominent victims killed with extraordinary ferocity. Respectable people, however, shunned publicity ("the Victorian standard for a true lady suggests, that one's name should appear in a newspaper only three times in one's life: birth, marriage and death"), so after the initial unavoidable headlines, editors may have been less inclined to print stories about Sperry and Umberfield, or perhaps their families were exerting their influence.[87] Many believed that Enoch Sperry's son, the Hon. Nehemiah Sperry, a wealthy businessman and Connecticut's secretary of state, was working behind the scenes.

On January 3, Charles Sanford provided a "tolerably straight account" of Mr. Umberfield's murder.[88] After confessing, he was apparently put quietly on trial, convicted of both crimes, and found legally responsible for his actions. On the face of it, Sanford is unlikely to have met any standard for sanity, yet he was sentenced to hang.

A reporter for the *New York Daily Times* visited the jail a few days after the double murder and was greeted by Sanford in cell number seventeen, who said, "Come here, oh come here thou Angel Michael. I recognized you in a moment." The prisoner wore an overcoat and a bloodstained shirt, and under his sealskin fur cap, both eyes were blackened. His face was bruised and cut from the farmers' cudgels and he spoke "rapidly but without passion," saying,

> "I am the Lord Emanuel and I am *Guyana Kana* [?]. I have eaten up what I had, and now you have come to release me from this place of misery; welcome thou Angel of the Lord. I could go to work, I am quite willing to go to work and be a boot-maker with I. W. Wooding [Wooding was a cobbler] (the man who was discharged of the MATTHEWS murder.)" He then showed me two rings that he had on his fingers, and said that "these are my signs and when I sign you with these then you shall be saved for God knows the seal of the Lord Emanuel. You are Michael, and will be saved. You are one of my men, and will be saved. You are one of my men, and I will save. I love you, and you shall go with me to the heaven of bliss when I go, and I am going directly. B-l-o-o-d, blood, blood, blood, who would not have blood?—blood is cheap, it flows freely, and its color is bright . . .

And so on. When the correspondent left, Sanford called out, "If the Angel Michael leaves me will the Lord leave me too?" Those who considered his madness self-evident attributed the death sentence to Nehemiah Sperry but Sanford never hanged. He already had "every appearance of being far gone with consumption" and six months after the murders was dead from tuberculosis or smallpox.[90] This gave rise to even more sinister rumors that his death was "helped along" by the contents of a "Black Bottle."[91] Murders, however, often give rise to strange stories. It was also claimed,

> [b]y those who were in a position to know . . . [t]hat it was the skeletal remains of none other than Charlie Sanford who for many years afterward, stood as an example of Primitive Man in an anthropological display at the Peabody Museum in New Haven . . .[92]

In fact, Yale's Peabody Museum (founded 1866) *did* have two human skeletons, and one was displayed in the primate evolution exhibit as an example of Homo sapiens, yet neither came from a Caucasian male; one was female and the other Chinese. Sanford's bones could not have gone to Yale's College Cabinet Museum, which was dedicated to minerals, corals, and fossils.[93] If the reader does not mind speculation piled on supposition, however, another explanation is possible.

The cadavers of executed criminals were often given to medical schools for dissection, and a specimen that displayed uncommon features like a clubfoot or curious skull was more likely to be preserved in a collection. Nineteenth-century scientists had a passion for gathering and measuring skulls (some museums still have hundreds squirreled away in their anthropology departments), and a protruding "prognathic" jaw was considered an apelike trait characteristic of primitive men, exactly what might be expected from someone who committed shockingly brutal crimes. (At the beginning of the twentieth century, the influential Italian criminologist Cesare Lombroso argued that habitual criminals were a less evolved form of humanity that display archaic physical features called *atavisms*.) So, while Sanford's skeleton most likely did *not* end up labeled "primitive man," the idea that it *could have* reflects contemporary thinking.

Enoch Sperry was buried on January 11, 1856, in the Westville Cemetery at New Haven, and his epitaph reads, "God knew the time and place to call his servant home."[94] Mr. Umberfield's grave can be found at Bethany's Sperry Cemetery. On January 3, 1856, he was laid under an upright gray slab reading:

IN

memory of

ICHABOD UMBERFIELD

Who was murdered

By a maniac

Jn'y 1, 1856.

Æ. 71.

A mournful New Year's Day
To my surviving their friends.
How sudden I am called away
Soon as the year begins.

County Jail

Thankful Hersey and Mrs. Wakeman shared a cell at the New Haven County Jail, and though God's Messenger was often sick in bed, she managed to compose a letter addressed to the "ministers of the world." It catalogs Amos Hunt's misdeeds and her suffering, interspersed with threats, whining, and an exposition of humankind's collective guilt with regard to her situation:

> I have plead [*sic*] with ministers and lawyers, and those in public office to take up my cause and bring to light this cruel murder [a reference to either the "spiritual murder" of the world or the attempt on her life; not the death of Justus Matthews]; but no one has stood for my defense, and in this way the whole world has become guilty of my death before God. A short time now remains in which this work may be done and the whole world saved. O! there is no one that will come up to the help of the Lord against this mighty Man of Sin, who has killed the whole world spiritually with his unseen power brought from the bottomless pit.[95]

In another letter enumerating Hunt's evils she calls him "a liar for he promised his Savior that he would never leave or forsake him; *that he would have his head taken off before he would do it*" [my italics].[96] This suggests that the full or near decapitations of Matthews, Sperry, and Umberfield were inspired by some aspect of the prophetess's teachings.[97] (On a lighter note, Mrs. Wakeman "advised the readers of Greeley's 'Tribune' to brew themselves an occasional cup of tea made from the bark of a witch-hazel tree in order to keep their bodies free from evil spirits. And as a result of this advice which was given some notice in the press several enterprising merchants in New York added this item to their stocks.")[98]

Sammy was also talking to the press. He explained aspects of their faith, such as salvation through Rhoda Wakeman ("At the first there were on the face of the earth, Adam, Eve and the Devil. It was the lie told by the devil, believed by the woman, and obeyed by the man, that caused the fall from immortality to death; and so now this happy time of the redemption must be in likeway brought about through a woman").[99] Like Mrs. Wakeman, Sly could not stop talking about Amos Hunt and the financial settlement, which "took the resurrection of everlasting life and changed it into damnation . . . by the payment of the five hundred dollars in recompensing damages for his attempted poisoning." Hunt's malice was exceptional even among Men of Sin, for "[b]y the payment of that money he bound the Saviour under it, and this has never been done before, wicked though former 'men of sin' had been."[100] Yet for all of Amos Hunt's evil, Sammy declared that the Wakemanites had no intention of harming him and wanted to expel the evil spirit through constant prayer.

Sly also mentioned groups similar, or sympathetic, to the Wakemanites "who entertain the faith, not yet perhaps perfected among them, but nearly sure." He counted among them the Irvingites, or Catholic Apostolic Church, an English sect whose members spoke in tongues, and Margaret Bishop of the Christian Israelites in New York City, a sect active throughout the English-speaking world that followed the teachings of British visionary John Wroe. Sammy stated that the Christian Israelites "carry out fully our views and meet for prayer such as we had. MRS. BISHOP was much interested in my sister and called on her several times and they frequently conversed on these matters."[101] Margaret Bishop responded promptly in a letter to the editor.

> Sir, you will certainly do me the justice as an individual, and the Christian Israelite members in general, by contradicting the assertion made in your print of Monday last. I never was in sympathy with these people—never had any "interest" in MRS. WAKEMAN. I accidentally saw her in New-Haven about thirteen years ago, and decidedly considered her insane.[102]

God's Messenger on Trial

The trio was back in court on January 17, when the grand jury found a true bill of murder against Samuel Sly and indicted Thankful Hersey and Rhoda Wakeman as accessories before and after the fact (no attempt was made to link Justus Matthews's death with the Sperry-Umberfield murders). Josiah Jackson and Abigail Sables were discharged from prison and the prophetess wept upon learning that she had to remain; Thankful Hersey pointed a finger at the old lady, who was sobbing under heavy veils, and announced, "They little know what they are about shutting up that person."[103]

Mrs. Wakeman declared that the world would end before they were tried; "she should" however, "permit us all to live on a little longer on probation, but she should bring judgment day when she got ready to do so."[104]

Three months later, on Wednesday, April 16, Judges Hinman and Waldo were presiding over the Wakemanites' trial in the Superior Court at New Haven. District attorney E. K. Foster and John D. Candee represented the state of Connecticut, while Joseph Sheldon Jr. and the Hon. Henry Dutton defended the prisoners.

The courtroom was crowded; every seat and all the standing room was taken, and proceedings began with a plea of "not guilty." Governor Dutton did not dispute that the defendant killed Matthews, or that the others were accessories to the crime, but "the defence would give conclusive evidence that those persons, at the time the murder was committed, were laboring under an insane delusion."[105] As for the state, when someone is murdered for being the Antichrist, prosecutors often argue that a more conventional motive was involved, such as jealousy, revenge, or, greed. In this case, their contention might have been that Matthews borrowed $200 from a savings association, loaned the money to Mrs. Wakeman, and was killed so they would not have to repay it. The question then became "how much pecuniary interest these parties had in getting Matthews out of the way."[106] To make a plausible argument, the state had to demonstrate that Mrs. Wakeman would kill for money, but if that was the plan they did not press it.

According to the prophetess she got nothing from Matthews except "a few vegetables, a few apples, and a small piece or two of salt pork," while Sammy claimed that the victim still owed him money for clothes; nevertheless, "I have never made a claim against him, for I loved him very much and wished him to be freed from sin."[107] No one seemed to know what Matthews did with the $200, and the Wakemanites accepted none of Hunt's $500 settlement money; they were so poor that Mrs. Wakeman said she "was obliged to sell my best feather bed to get money to pay my rent," and even then, Ephraim Lane testified, "she would always give away everything she had."[108]

The first day of the trial was dedicated to establishing the facts of the case. Jurors saw a floor plan of the Beaver Street house, heard Matthews's injuries described, and heard the Wakemanites testify about events on the night of the murder. Sheriff Parmalee related the particulars of Sammy's confession and displayed the physical evidence, including the knife and bloody clothing. The state rested that afternoon, and the remainder of the first day was given over to testimony about the defendants' strange beliefs and behavior.

Witnesses included Phebe A. Beckwith, a former Wakemanite who was declared an unbeliever after Mrs. Wakeman "began to talk so much about this enchantment which I could not believe." When Beckwith last visited the prophetess, "Uncle Sammy shut himself up in the closet, he was so afraid of me."[109] With that, court adjourned till the next day, when there was more testimony in the same vein, including a baker who told how the Wakemanites "had an idea that my bread . . . was enchanted and that anyone who ate it would die."[110] Friends and relatives took the stand, followed by experts who had evaluated the defendants' mental conditions.

Drs. Worthington Hooker, Jonathan Knight, Jerome C. Smith, Pliny A. Jewett, and Mrs. Wakeman's own physician, E. C. Chamberlain, had some differences of opinion, yet none considered the accused competent. Sly was a weak-minded imbecile, possibly a monomaniac, or suffering from dementia; Dr. Hooker thought that when Sammy killed Matthews "there was an intense excitement in the house, and I think if he had any consciousness that he was doing a wrong act, the consciousness was very slight."[111] Miss Hersey's mind, though strong, was wholly given over to Mrs. Wakeman, and she had two relatives who went mad. Mrs. Wakeman was insane, or nearly so, and Dr. Smith believed "from the evidence adduced that her disease has considerably increased within two or three years." Dr. Jewett doubted the sincerity of Mrs. Wakeman's beliefs, but this was a minority view; few questioned the depth of her convictions.

Ephraim Lane said, "You might as well try to move the West Rock [a mountain ridge and local landmark] as to reason her out of her delusions; I have heard ministers speak with her about them, and they said it was no use to talk to her . . ."[112] He also had "no doubt but that the old lady got her mind so wrought up that it did really hurt her when a person came whom she thought had a bad spirit."[113]

By the end of day two, with all the evidence pointing in the same direction, the Hon. Henry Dutton asked District Attorney Foster if he would seek a verdict *other than* not guilty on the grounds of insanity. The prosecutor replied that he did not feel authorized by the evidence to claim any other, for "[t]he case had assumed an aspect not contemplated by him at its commencement."[114] Moreover, he "did not consider it necessary to sum up the evidence, and was willing to let the case go to the jury without argument."[115] With both sides in accord, Judge Hinman rose and told the jurors "they might retire and bring in such a verdict as they thought was right, and such as justice required," adding that the Court had the power to make an order for the further confinement of the prisoners.[116] The men rose and left the courtroom for ten minutes of deliberation before returning with a verdict.

Between Sly's mental limitations, Hersey's fanaticism, and their utter faith in an unbalanced woman, the defendants were found not guilty on the grounds of insanity. Mrs. Wakeman and Sammy wept as they heard the verdict, while Miss Hersey seemed troubled at being considered insane.

Judge Hinman left the bench and the public began leaving the courtroom when Judge Waldo rose and instructed the sheriff "'to return these prisoners to jail, where they will be confined until further orders from this Court, or until they are discharged by due process of law.'"[117]

Denouement

Their destination was the sprawling Hartford Retreat, then Connecticut's only institution for the destitute insane (it is now the Institute for Living); Thankful Hersey was more fortunate. During the trial, the Court received a number of depositions from Worcester and Auburn, Massachusetts, testifying to her excellent character, and a Mr. Samuel A. Foote "gave the requisite bonds for the protection of the community against her, and took her to his house . . ."[118] There she did plain sewing and other light work until her death on May 12, 1857.[119] Sammy was at the asylum for ten years and in that time came to believe that he was the prophet Elijah. Eventually he stopped eating and drinking and died of starvation on July 14, 1865. By then the prophetess had been dead six years.

Rhoda Wakeman made her second and last trip to heaven in 1859 when "the prophetess passed on once again into the white clouds of the hereafter—free, one may hope, from evil spirits and sin."[120]

Amos Hunt: Psychic Detective

With the exception of Amos Hunt, nothing more was heard from her followers, who returned to ordinary pursuits like peddling and shoemaking. The former Man of Sin, however, became a clairvoyant (it is given as his "Profession, Occupation or Trade" in the census of 1880). Hunt's purported psychic abilities led to him playing a minor role in "the most mysterious of all the cases which have baptized Connecticut in blood": the death of Mary Stannard.[121]

Every era has its favorite kinds of murders, and for nineteenth-century Americans, it was the innocent woman seduced by a respectable man, preferably a clergyman, who kills her to avoid scandal. As the mother of an illegitimate child, twenty-two-year-old Mary Stannard was not the ideal virginal victim, but her good nature and naïveté attracted the Rev. Herbert H. Hayden, a married man with a family, and Mary found herself pregnant again.

On September 3, 1878, her body was found lying on a path

in Rockland, Connecticut. The postmortem revealed that Mary Stannard, who was *not* pregnant, had been poisoned, beaten, and stabbed (Dr. Pliny A. Jewett, who examined Charles Sanford's victims, assisted at Mary Stannard's autopsy), and since the Rev. Hayden was known to have recently purchased arsenic, he was arrested.

It was a long and contentious trial, and, as it progressed, "Dr. [Amos] Hunt," a "medical clairvoyant" at Fair Haven, was hired to find out what happened. For two dollars, he went into a trance and "minutely described the scene of the murder, the victim and the murderer and what led to the commission of the crime." According to Hunt, Hayden stunned Mary Stannard with a rock, and as she lay there,

> a gleam of hate shot across his face, and approaching her, he turned over and looked at her, then he quickly put his hand in his pocket, drew out his clasp-knife, and after pulling back his shirt sleeves to the shoulder [he had no coat on] he turned her head carefully to one side, and without a moment's hesitation, plunged the knife blade into her neck.[122]

Hunt's narrative, with its echoes of Justus Matthews's murder, appears as *The Clairvoyant's Wonderful Story*, part of the 1879 pamphlet *Poor Mary Stannard!*

The trial of Herbert H. Hayden ended in a hung jury, so he was released and soon left the ministry to return to his former trade of carpentry. Amos Hunt presumably continued his psychic medical practice, and the murder of Mary Stannard remains unsolved.

An Obsolete Atrocity

In the 2002 documentary *The Manson Women*, Associated Press reporter Lisa Deutsch describes Charles Manson's "Family" as the United States' "first real cult," and the murders they committed as the "first cult killings we know of in this country."[123] They were not, of course, but the Wakemanites' crimes, like the Tate-LaBianca murders, became the standard example of cult fanaticism for generations of Americans.

When Charles F. Freeman of Pocasset, Massachusetts, imitated Abraham's near sacrifice of Isaac by stabbing his five-year-old daughter Edith to death in 1879, the "Pocasset Horror" was compared to the Wakemanite murders.[124] Wakemaniteism also represented unorthodox sects' *potential* for violence.

In the 1880s, two sisters who had achieved "perfection" and were both inhabited by the spirit of Jesus Christ, led a group of about forty disciples called the "Martinites" at Cincinnati, Ohio. They had done nothing wrong, yet were compared to the Wakemanites for their members were considered likely to "become assassins if the crazy woman who is to them the Deity should tell them to remove a few citizens of Cincinnati."[125]

Ninety-seven years after Justus Matthews's throat was cut, "Wakemanites" still appeared in the *Encyclopedia Americana*, as "certain fanatics who were supposed to be harmless until they committed a murder at New Haven, Conn., in 1855."[126] Today they are almost forgotten. This can be attributed to the passage of time, and cult murders in the second half of the twentieth-century, including Manson's Family, the People's Temple at Jonestown, and Heaven's Gate, that spilled enough blood to wash away memories of the Wakemanites from everywhere except the place it happened.

Legacy

Mr. Umberfield's death has become part of local legend. The house where he died was by Lake Watrous and burned down after Sanford's rampage (another house built on the site is sometimes identified as Umberfield's), but the popular belief is that he was killed at a more northern section of the Downs Road, toward Hamden.

It is an unpaved track that runs through an appropriately eerie stretch of woods, and is visited by hikers and teenagers who try to scare themselves. In addition to an historical axe murder, the area is supposed to be swarming with ghosts, demonic children, hydrocephalic cannibal mutants ("melon-heads"), and a Bigfoot-like monster called the Downs Road Creature, making it a natural destination for "legend tripping."

North American society has few of the formal rites of passage that mark an adolescent's transition to adulthood in traditional societies, so informal ones like legend tripping have appeared. It consists of visiting places with a reputation for being haunted, maybe performing a simple ritual (such as shining headlights or walking around a tombstone), and often ends in headlong flight. Legend trips give young people an opportunity to "tell stories, demonstrate their courage, and possibly experience some of the rumored manifestations of supernatural events associated with the site,"[127] as well as connecting them to the community's past.

For teenagers hunting melon-heads or the Downs Road creature, this includes a memory of the Wakemanite's homicidal madness that lingers along one dark and leafy path through the woods of Connecticut.

The Littlest Stigmatic

On March 17, 1972, Cloretta Robertson, "Cocoa" to her friends, sat in a fifth-grade classroom at Oakland, California's Santa Fe Elementary School.[1] It was an ordinary day that anyone who attended fifth grade can imagine: rows of children in different stages of drowsiness, a big clock on the wall that seems to run slower than ordinary clocks and the mingled aroma of chalk dust, peanut butter, and bologna that is the smell of primary education. Shannon Bremmond Sr., the teacher, stands in front of the room revealing the mysteries of photosynthesis or long division, or whatever was on the lesson plan that day, while Cloretta probably gathered wool. She was a bright but indifferent student whose main interest was religion.

Her family belonged to the small church down the street from the school, New Light Baptist, where Cloretta sang in the choir and was a junior usher.[2] She was an unusually devout ten-year-old who peppered her conversation with scriptural references and spent many afternoons reading the Bible and Christian literature. A week earlier she had finished the book *Crossroads* by John Webster, which "was deeply religious with emotional overtones"; then, on March 13, she watched a movie on television about the Passion and had a vivid dream about the Crucifixion that night. She often dreamed about the Bible, and Good Friday was two weeks away, which presumably contributed to what would be a memorable day at Santa Fe ("Holy Faith") Elementary.[3]

Blood appeared in the palm of her left hand. A friend noticed that she was bleeding and informed Cloretta, whose first thought was, "I had cut myself."[4] Mr. Bremmond saw the blood too, and wiped it away, but it continued flowing; the source was not evident and he sent Cloretta to see Susan Carson, the school nurse. She examined the little girl's hand and later told a newspaper reporter:

> "Her palms were bleeding when she first came in," Mrs. Carlson said. "There isn't any evidence of a wound. It was fresh blood. I wiped it off and after a while . . . it would appear again . . . there were no puncture wounds. I looked with a magnifying glass."[5]

When the history of elementary school nursing is written, look for Mrs. Carson as the first of her profession to see a case of stigmata.

Holy Marks

Stigmata is the plural form of *stigma*, the Latin word for branding, burning permanent marks into the skin with a hot iron, and it is used to describe wounds, blisters, or bleeding that spontaneously appear at the same places they were suffered by Jesus. The stigmata take different forms, but they often occur on the extremities where nails were hammered into Jesus's hands and feet, and the torso where a Roman soldier delivered the coup de grâce with a spear. There can be stripes from flagellation, punctures on the forehead caused by thorns, knees abraded from the three falls on the road to Calvary, even a shoulder bruised from carrying the cross. Other forms of stigmata are not directly related to the Passion, such as shedding tears of blood, a cross-shaped wound on the forehead, even a "ring" that appears on the finger of female stigmatics who have "contracted betrothals or a marriage with our Lord."[6] There are also "spiritual stigmata." These are invisible and allowed saints like Catherine of Siena (1347–1380) to experience the pain of the phenomenon without external signs.

It began more than a century before St. Catherine's time, in 1224, with St. Francis of Assisi (1182–1226). He was engaged in "peaceful ecstasies of contemplation" on La Verna, a hill near Assisi, Italy, when a six-winged seraph appeared, bearing a cross with the crucified Christ.[7] Many artists have depicted the scene, using golden beams of light to connect

Jesus's wounds to the places on Francis's body where he developed a singular form of stigmata described by St. Bonaventure in the *Life of Saint Francis* (1261):

> For his hands and feet seemed to be pierced through the midst with nails, the heads of the nails shewing in the palms of the hands, and upper side of the feet, and their points shewing on the other side; the heads of the nails were round and black in the hands and feet, while the points were long, bent, and as it were turned back, being formed of the flesh itself, and protruding therefrom. The right side, moreover was—as if it had been pierced by a lance—seamed with a ruddy scar, wherefrom ofttimes welled the sacred blood, staining his habit and breeches.[8]

There have been around 330 pious Roman Catholic stigmatics since then, of which more than 60 are beatified or canonized.[9] By itself, the phenomenon does not indicate unusual holiness, and seemingly authentic cases have occurred in hysterics, the conventionally religious, and, in rare cases, non-Catholics. Moreover, the church is reluctant to proclaim *anything* miraculous. Even a popular figure like the Italian stigmatic Padre Pio (later St. Pio of Pietrelcina), was suspected of being a "mad . . . self-mutilating psychopath possessed of the devil who exploited people's credulity."[10] It took a half century of investigation for Pio's case to be recognized as supernatural.

Pope Benedict XIV (1675–1758) established guidelines for assessing the stigmata, distinguishing between wounds that are "natural, supernatural and preternatural (or else human, divine or diabolical)," and noting the characteristics of heavenly stigmata. They are:

> (i) sudden in appearance, (ii) [involve] major tissue modifications, (iii) persistence and inalterability despite all therapy, (iv) hemorrhage, (v) absence of infection or suppuration [some wounds even give off a perfumed smell], (vi) sudden and perfect disappearance . . .[11]

None of this was of immediate importance to Cloretta Robertson. When a little girl is black, Baptist, and bleeding from her palms like Jesus, the first priority is seeing a doctor. An appointment was made to see a hematologist on March 20.

Children's Hospital

Four days after it began, Cloretta's right palm was bleeding. Two days after that it was her left foot, and on the seventh day her right foot and right side of the thorax; when she got the crown-of-thorns stigmata on the fourteenth day, she bled from the middle of her forehead. The bleeding occurred one to five times daily, mostly from the hands, and the different places did not bleed at the same time. When asked about it, she replied shyly, "'It happens. It just sort of comes on, I don't know before. It doesn't hurt. I just look down and it's there. I don't know what it is.'"[12] She also thought, "'It's weird.'"[13]

At the Children's Hospital Medical Center the staff hematologist watched Cloretta for two hours through a one-way glass but saw nothing unusual. It was only when she returned from the ladies' room that he saw "dried blood on her lower right chest." There was also "a relatively excoriated area on the front of her tongue—reactive and red—which could be sign of bleeding there."[14] Medical tests found no physical disorders, or anything in her family history that might be relevant to stigmata, such as blood diseases, cases of prolonged bleeding, easy bruising, or mental illness. Her background was also fairly normal.

Born June 2, 1961, Cloretta was the last of six children born to her mother, Alice. Alice Calhoun was thirty-six years old at the time and not married to Cloretta's father, who lived in Oakland but had almost no contact with his daughter. In 1966, Alice wedded her third husband, fifty-five-year-old Andrew Robertson, and between his job as a longshoreman and Alice's as a dental technician, Cloretta led a "lower middle-class" life with "her parents, three brothers, a sister, three nieces and a nephew in a big house" on 54th Street at Oakland.[15]

The hematologist was evidently skeptical, but no one in the Robertson family seemed to doubt the reality of what was happening. When Cloretta's forehead became speckled with blood (crown-of-thorns stigmata), they photographed it and gave the pictures to reporters. Meanwhile, Alice Robertson worried about Cloretta's health and her long-term prospects, saying tearfully, "I just don't know how this will affect the rest of her life."[16] Getting treatment for stigmata also proved difficult. "It's been a real trial for me," she said, "going from doctor to doctor and taking her to hospitals in the middle of the night and having people there look at me like I'm crazy."[17] She eventually had to walk Cloretta to school to fend off the curious; in fact, the person who seemed most excited about the phenomenon was their pastor.

At Church

On March 23, the Rev. Leonard L. Hester described what was happening to the congregation and delivered a sermon about Cloretta; the story was attracting so much attention that it appeared in the religion section of *Jet*.

The article, *Child's Easter Bleeding Puzzles Parents, Doctors*, is as straightforward as the title and illustrated with photographs of the Robertsons at home. We see a serene Cloretta seated on the sofa next to her mother, flanked by Rev. and Mrs. Hester. There is Cloretta standing before an image of the Sacred Heart of Jesus, reading a letter from a girl in San Francisco (the Sacred Heart is an unusual image for a Baptist household; perhaps *Jet*'s photographer brought it as a prop for the pictures). We also see Cloretta taking part in ordinary activities, like getting ready to dye Easter eggs with her nieces, Frances, Sonya, and Tonya. This was important; Andrew Robertson made a point of saying that, stigmata aside, "his daughter is an otherwise normal girl who likes to watch television and play with her friends."[18] Her stepfather might have also encouraged Cloretta's seemingly detached response to the phenomenon.

She was very calm and said of the bleeding, "It happens. I don't feel happy or sad, just in-between."[19] Mr. Robertson said, "I've been worrying about my baby and trying to keep her from getting excited."[20] He added that Cloretta "doesn't get upset (by the bleeding). It's almost as if she doesn't mind. Sometimes we'll be playing, she'll just look down and say, 'Pop, there it is,' and there's the blood."[21]

The doctors "tentatively diagnosed her as suffering from 'Easter bleeding syndrome'" and the Robertsons hoped it would end with the holiday.[22] "If the bleeding does not stop after Easter," Andrew Robertson said, "we may have to do something further."[23]

In addition to the hematologist, doctors Loretta F. Early of the Department of Pediatrics, West Oakland Health Center, and Joseph E. Lifschutz from the Department of Psychiatry, University of California, Berkeley, saw Cloretta; there were several visits and the pair later coauthored "A Case of Stigmata" for the *Archives of General Psychiatry.*[24]

Second Opinions

The journal article discusses stigmata and psychogenic purpura, a rare disorder, in which bruises are created by the patient's emotions. It also considers Cloretta's background, physical and mental health, and the reality of spontaneous bleeding.

The doctors' initial impression of their patient was of a

> pleasant, neatly and attractively groomed prepubescent black girl, cheerful, friendly, and somewhat reserved in her conversations with adult white men. With one of us (L.F.E. [Dr. Early]), however, she was much more spontaneous and conversed freely and openly. Her physical examination results were entirely normal; she was and remained alert, well-oriented, and a pleasant patient.

She considered herself "shy, desirous of getting along with people, happy, and feeling that she had little to offer others," while

> [h]er family describes her as gregarious, likeable, active, creative, happy, and very helpful in household chores. Her teacher described her as talkative, gregarious, and somewhat manipulative. We believe that the family was very close, warm, positive, and apparently emotionally and

> physically healthy. We wondered, however, about the effect on the children of considerable overcrowding in the home. We lacked considerable information about pertinent family such as whether she was ever exposed to scenes of violence or to excessive sexual stimulation [experiences associated with cases of psychogenic bruising]. It is notable that both the patient and her mother had strong positive feelings about the sense of intimacy with the many family members in the home.

There "was no apparent conflict over her natural father," and as for her religious life, New Light Baptist Church was "mildly fundamentalist, with minimal emphasis on hellfire and brimstone, accentuating positive aspects of Christianity and good works."[25] Her life was not a hothouse for psychopathologies, and Cloretta did not

> appear to have a hysterical personality. She was not self-centered, overly dramatic, flirtatious, impetuous, excitable, or manifesting any obvious neurotic symptoms. The only hint of neurotic symptoms was her casual attitude toward the bleeding, a bit of "la belle indifference."[26]

This apparent unconcern might have proved useful, however, for a child trying to chart a course between her mother's fears and her pastor's excitement. The most worrisome aspect of the case were incidents of auditory hallucinations, which began a few days before the bleeding started and occurred when Cloretta was praying at bedtime.

Her prayer consisted of a blessing to each individually named family member. The hallucination consisted of a simple, positive, brief instruction such as, "Your prayers will be answered."

In addition, there were voices talking to her (once on Good Friday and again on Easter Sunday), telling her to go and pray with certain people. She did so, believing that her prayers would have healing power, and in each case they did. After Easter Sunday, though, the voices stopped and there were no visual hallucinations.

As for the stigmata itself, the inevitable question is whether or not it was really happening, and could "self-induced wounding [be] ruled out as the cause of these strange phenomena?"[27]

Physical Evidence

There have been a number of fraudulent stigmatics. The sixteenth-century nun Maria de la Visitacion was caught painting stigmata onto her skin ("Her physicians defended her, but the Inquisition's examiners scrubbed away her wounds to reveal unblemished skin"), as well as more complicated cases in which subjects were not consciously aware of wounding themselves.[28]

One of the most prominent modern stigmatics, Therese

Neumann (1898–1962) of Konnersreuth, Germany, experienced a wide variety of phenomena including spectacularly gruesome displays of bleeding. They went on for decades, but apparently no one ever actually saw the bleeding begin; moreover, in the years before the stigmata appeared, she suffered from convulsions during which "'[t]he fingers trembled, and she dug them into her palms.'"[29] Skepticism is inevitable in cases where the stigmatic must be alone, unobserved, or concealed in bedclothes for blood to start flowing, and had Cloretta's episodes always been preceded by a visit to the ladies' room, as happened at the Children's Hospital, it would have raised suspicions. Witnesses, however, saw the bleeding begin while she sat in class, or carefully inspected her hand as more blood appeared, without finding an opening in the skin.

During Cloretta's first trip to the hospital, Dr. Early attended to her hand in a way that suggested blood was passing through Cloretta's unbroken skin. The doctor told a reporter, "'I have wrapped her hands thoroughly and the blood was there after 18 hours. There was no way she could have removed the bandages [and] then replaced them, or stuck an object beneath them to insert any blood.'"[30] The formal account in "A Case of Stigmata" states that Cloretta's left hand was

> bound thoroughly with an elastoplast boxing glove dressing. . . . She was returned to school and within

> three hours, while in the classroom, bled spontaneously from her right palm. The bandage was removed by the school staff the following day so that she could play her clarinet and blood was reported in the dressing."[31]

Drs. Early and Lifschutz never saw Cloretta start bleeding; she claimed not to know when it was going to happen, yet good luck and insight into how the phenomenon might be triggered, allowed Dr. Early to see the stigmata occurring and examine the skin afterward.

The single most important factor in precipitating the phenomenon seems to have been Cloretta's "identification with the figure of Christ. She was also preoccupied with Christ's suffering . . ."[32] When interviewed, she "denied any knowledge of the stigmata phenomenon prior to bleeding," yet also "recognizes that her bleeding is connected with the death of Christ, celebrated nine days from now on Good Friday."[33] "It was only after the first week of bleeding that she learned of St. Francis of Assisi and later clearly identified with him."[34] So, on Cloretta's fifth visit to Dr. Early's office,

> the physician suggested that she sit in the examination room next to her office and draw pictures of St. Francis of Assisi from a book she had brought with her. The patient was alone, nursing staff was on lunch break, and while copying pictures she noticed bleeding from her left palm. She immediately returned to the physician's office with

two to three drops of blood in the palm of her left hand. The physician observed the blood to increase in volume four fold, welling up from the center of the palm and spreading over the palmar creases. After wiping the wet blood away no lesions were present with the exception of a pea-sized bluish discoloration remaining in the palm of her left hand for approximately three minutes."[35]

In 1975, Dr. Early described the phenomenon as "red blood cells . . . passing through the walls of tiny capillaries and through the skin."[36] (The blood was also analyzed.[37]) As far as the reality of Cloretta's stigmata was concerned, the doctors noted that "[s]elf-induced trauma is almost humanly impossible to rule out absolutely in such cases; but we believe the likelihood of it to be almost nil in this case." They continued, "One can no longer dispute the power of mental and emotional forces to control such physical phenomena. By analogy we need not doubt that profound, intense religious and emotional forces, conscious and unconscious, could cause stigmatic bleeding."[38]

They were not a product of hysteria; Dr. Lifschutz described Cloretta as "a very well-adjusted, stable little girl."[39] Nor was it psychogenic purpura, which are very rare and seen in people that have "severe hysterical and masochistic traits . . . [whose] life stories were checkered with violence, sadism, and sexual trauma."[40] In short, "[t]he only significant background for the stigmata was her religiosity"[41] and identification with Jesus's suffering.

As often happens with stigmata, the phenomenon reached its climax on Good Friday. Cloretta was staying at a friend's house that day and claimed that after waking up she bled from all six sites simultaneously for the first and only time ("there were [however] neither witnesses nor blood reported on the bed sheets").[42] After nineteen days, she felt "'it was all over.'"[43] But the doctors predicted that "the chances are better than even that she will again bleed at subsequent Easter seasons."[44]

At church that day, members of the press almost outnumbered the small congregation. The Rev. Hester delivered a sermon about the crucifixion and talked about Cloretta, calling the phenomenon a "miracle" and saying that "We pray for Cloretta and her family that this bleeding will be with her throughout her life." He told *Jet* that "[t]he Lord has prepared her for this," and as the congregation filed out she "shyly offered her hand to those leaving," for the Rev. Hester believed "'that by touching her hand we'll all be blessed.'"[45]

Like so many cases involving unexplained phenomena, there is no satisfying resolution to Cloretta's story.

The stigmata did not return during Easter 1973, just a "completely unsubstantiated report of one observer who claimed to have seen blood on one of her hands on one occasion . . ."[46] The following year a church service was held in Cloretta's honor on Palm Sunday with a benefit to raise money for her college education; she might have had a brief episode of bleeding on Good Friday, but in 1975 the phenomenon returned with its former intensity.

Services were just beginning at New Light Baptist on March 16, 1975, when thirteen-year-old Cloretta walked down the aisle to show her hand to the Rev. Hester. He turned her bleeding palm toward the congregation, and "[t]hey were so stunned, the pastor said, that it took 15 minutes for the people to regain their composure, so he could continue with the service."[47]

After three years, Alice Robertson seemed calmer about her daughter's peculiarity. Maybe she relaxed when the doctors decided it was not caused by a mental or physical illness, nor had it worsened. The stigmata were essentially a seasonal problem, something like hay fever, though there had reportedly been episodes during the summer as well (it would be interesting to know which books her daughter was reading, or what movies she saw, at the time). The press was invited to the Robertson home the next day (March 17), and when Cloretta's palm started bleeding at 11:20 A.M., they took pictures.

She appeared in the *Oakland Tribune* again on March 22, 1975, but this time it was on the page for church advertisements. There, among announcements for the Salvation Army's Citadel Songsters, and a Drive-In Worship Center at the Appian 80 Shopping Center, is an ad for the "Youth Supernatural End-Time Revival" presented by the East Oakland Faith Deliverance Center and New Light Baptist Church; it is illustrated with a photograph of Cloretta displaying the palm of her left hand. The copy includes a brief history of her stigmata and promises:

> **Supernatural Happenings at East Oakland Deliverance Center**
>
> Mass miracle healing services nightly. Bring the sick, troubled, the dope addict and the possessed, and depressed. Come expecting a miracle, for God will be moving by His spirit.
>
> Furthermore:
>
> Cloretta Starks will be present in each service.

(Healing gets a passing mention from the doctors, but Cloretta and the Rev. Hester emphasize it.)

She reportedly bled from all six sites again on Good Friday, 1975, but by then reporting about her stigmata had become routine, and the Rev. Hester had more to say about the revival, which reportedly attracted crowds of around 1,200. Cloretta bled during all but two of the meetings, and "miracle healings were claimed almost every night."[48]

Though she now used the name *Starks*, being a headliner at religious revivals does not seem to have changed Cloretta any more than the media attention. She was an eighth-grader whose favorite subject was math, she enjoyed sports, and, as might be expected in someone who sees "her life as dedicated to relieving suffering in others," she was planning to become a registered nurse.[49]

For the next two years, Cloretta appeared at the Youth Supernatural End-Time Revival and the stigmata returned at Easter time, usually during services at New Light Baptist Church. It might have become an annual event, but after 1977, when Mrs. Robertson told the *Oakland Tribune* that fifteen-year-old Cloretta's "health and spirits are good and that the girl has seen a doctor about the recurrence of the bleeding," the stories seem to stop.[50]

This may be a failure of research, but the lack of follow-ups or "where are they now" articles has led to speculation about her subsequent life.

Wounded

In Claudia Mair Burney's novel, *Wounded: A Love Story*, a priest tells the story of "Cloretta of Oakland, California" to a twenty-four-year-old black woman with stigmata. The events of 1972 are recounted more or less accurately before considering what might have happened afterward.

> The next Easter her family watched her carefully, but it never happened again. Or if it did, they didn't let on, and I can't blame them for that. She was a kid. You protect the defenseless.
>
> Cloretta Robinson [*sic*] drifted into obscurity. Like the high school I wrote about years ago, few people cared about a black juvenile stigmatic. But sometimes I wonder what became of the little girl who was marked with the passion wounds of Christ one Eastertide. I imagine she wondered why she was chosen, questioned both her sanity and sanctity, and maybe when she was older, and those years were from her, she wondered if she made the whole thing up.
>
> Then again, she could have died young, and her family let her rest in peace without the stain of stigmata to prick her eternal rest. Or perhaps she lived the rest of her life quietly healing the suffering and alleviating the pain of others through her prayers, knowing God so loved the ghetto, that he gave his only begotten Son, and left His mark on Cloretta to prove it.[51]

In fact, she still lives near Oakland, but what Burney calls a drift into obscurity might be someone who successfully reclaimed her privacy.

The Normalest Stigmatic

Cloretta is an anomaly among stigmatics. Beyond its unexpected appearance on someone of her age, race, and religion, there is a gulf of normality separating her from other cases. While they lay in bed bleeding on the sheets and radiating sanctity, Cloretta played basketball. (In fact, some stigmatics are not holy invalids. Father James Bruse, pastor of St. Frances de Sales Church at Kilmarnock, Virginia, is an active clergyman who experienced bleeding from 1991 to 1993 along with a variety of other phenomena. He is also a three-time world record holder for marathon roller-coaster riding.[52])

What became of her? When considering Cloretta Starks, it may be best to look for ordinary motivations. The bleeding could have stopped, she may have fallen in love, or perhaps identifying with St. Francis of Assisi drew her toward the Roman Catholic Church; one can imagine how its saints, mystics, and martyrs would appeal to a religious adolescent with bleeding palms.

Perhaps she simply went back to being "Cocoa," an unremarkable woman who goes to church with a layer of absorbent gauze under her immaculate white gloves. Just in case.

The Four Wild Men of Dr. Dedge

When Judge Braswell D. Deen Jr., retired head of the Georgia Court of Appeals, was young, he had a memorable face-to-face encounter with a wild man on the streets of Alma, Georgia.[1]

> I was about twelve years old, working at Quality Cash Store, sometimes called Greenways Grocery Store, in Alma, Ga. The store was located on the main street, 12th St. It was in the middle 30s. I was inside the store when we heard a large noise and growl coming down the street.
>
> We went outside and saw a pickup truck, which came by pulling a two-wheel cart containing a large cage containment with prisonlike bars; the wild man was inside roaring. As I remember, Albert Douglas, who was my boss, was laughing and said, there goes Dr. Dedge and his

> wild man . . . I actually saw and witnessed this, which was scary at my young age.[2]

Seeing a howling black man with two horns growing out of his head made an impression on Judge Deen, but who was Dr. Dedge, who was in the cage, and why were they driving around Georgia?

The answer involves economics, entertainment, folklore, science, and pseudoscience, all of which contributed to the creation of the "Okefenokee Wild Man."

Compound Beings

Human-animal hybrids have occupied an important place in our imaginations since at least the Paleolithic Age, when a deer-headed man with a rack of antlers and tail was painted on the walls of the cave of Trois Frères cave at Ariège, France. The figure, dubbed *"Le Sorcier,"* is first in a procession of extraordinary beings that continues today. Discoveries made on the island of Flores in 2003 prove that a "hybrid" of ape and human was not imaginary just eighteen thousand years ago, yet even without *Homo floresiensis*, every society has its beast-men and they serve a variety of purposes: gods (Pan), heroes (Enkidu), symbols of the wilderness (woodwoses), and uncataloged species of primates (Bigfoot), each of which reflects a somewhat different worldview.

Science, of course, has been shaping the Western outlook since the eighteenth century, and while cartographers stopped labeling unexplored sections of the map "here be monsters," explorers and settlers kept encountering them. The nineteenth and early twentieth centuries produced many reports of primitive, not quite human, beings, and these were incorporated into new intellectual frameworks such as medicine or anthropology.

Where a medieval traveler might have returned from Africa with tales of Ethiopian unicorn men, the Victorian Army surgeon wrote an article titled "Horned Men on Africa: Further Particulars of Their Existence" for the December 10, 1887, issue of the *British Medical Journal*, in which he describes three unrelated West Africans with the same remarkable "well-marked bony exostosis or knob-like growth of the infra-orbital ridges of the maxillary bones," a kind of crossbeam between the nostrils and eyes.

Likewise, when Col. Percy Fawcett was passing through Brazil's Cordilheira dos Parecis in 1914, he encountered the Maricoxi, a tribe of "large, hairy men, with exceptionally long arms, and with foreheads sloping back from pronounced eye ridges, men of a very primitive kind, in fact, and stark naked." For naturalist Ivan Sanderson, the Maricoxi were not a mystery but living representatives of a "neanderthaloid-type Submen living in the Matto Grosso."[3] Nor were beings like these restricted to distant and exotic places; American newspapers were once filled with accounts of "wild men."

It was a catchall term applied to lunatics, hermits, and monsters, whether it was the 1883 sighting at Morganville, Georgia, of someone with "a sack round his head" who "has been seen to eat dead animals and wraps himself in horse hide" or the man captured swimming from island to island in Georgia's Ocheecee Swamp, "destitute of clothing, emaciated, and covered with a phenomenal growth of hair."[4] There were also beings like the "wild man of Lookout Point," which would now be called "Bigfoot." The witness, a "reliable gentleman," said it stood "about 7 or 7½ feet high, hairy as an old bear, and would weigh, from his looks, 400 pounds; had a pole in one hand that looked to be about ten feet long, which he handles as easy as a stout healthy man would a pipestem. His name was asked, and the answer came in the shape of a large stone, which weighed at least 100 pounds."[5]

Wild men fascinated the public, and exhibitors from P. T. Barnum to the proprietor of the lowliest mud show, set out to satisfy that curiosity for the price of a ticket.

At the Sideshow

The sideshow's heyday lasted 110 years (1840–1950), and for ten of those eleven decades they were a staple of "dime museums, circuses, fairs, amusement parks, and carnivals."[6] Wild people were usually "pitshows," in which members of the audience:

entered a tent with an eight by ten foot diameter enclosure in the center in which they could walk around. Down in the pit would be the wild person, moaning and snarling at the spectators. If there were snakes in the pit, the wild person might poke at them to provoke hissing sounds.[7]

Looking into the hole, visitors saw a dark-skinned and dirty savage with protruding fangs and long matted hair, dressed in rags, or an animal skin, with maybe some bone ornaments. Wild people ate raw meat or, in the lowest kinds of exhibits, bit the heads off live animals ("glomming geeks"), but most shows relied on the wild man's acting ability.

They were a popular, if modest, attraction that had little in common with the original sideshow wild men discovered:

In the Island of Borneo, beneath an Eastern sky
Just under the Equator, with mountains towering high,
Where roves the wild Ouran-Outang, Gorilla and Malay,
And beasts of fiercest nature are watching for their prey . . .[8]

Like most wild people, they were captured by a group of armed men after a gory and dramatic struggle and then brought to civilization, where "Waino" and "Plutano," the "Wild Men of Borneo," first appeared on stage around 1850.

The pair stood three and a half feet tall and weighed forty-five pounds each (their tombstone at Mound View

Cemetery, Mt. Vernon, Ohio, reads "LITTLE MEN"), yet these "Modern Sampsons [*sic*]" lifted heavy weights and even members of the audience, spoke gibberish, and recited poetry to demonstrate how civilization had lifted them above their former barbarous condition.[9] They were, in fact, American brothers named Hiram (1825–1905) and Barney (1827–1912) Davis, whose size, strength, and goatlike, bearded faces suggested a blurring of boundaries between man and beast that became more pronounced in future wild men influenced by the popularity of Charles Darwin's *On the Origin of Species* in 1859.

Darwin's book made concepts like evolution and natural selection part of Western thinking and added a scientific gloss to wild people. Someone like Krao Farini, a Thai woman with hypertrichosis (excessive growth of hair) was not just advertised as strange or exotic but as a scientifically important "missing link," "Darwin's Human Monkey."

Likewise, posters for the most famous wild man, "Zip the Pinhead" or the "What-Is-It?" called him the "connecting link between the WILD NATIVE AFRICAN AND THE ORANG OUTANG," with handbills claiming that he was captured in Africa by "a party of adventurers . . . in search of the Gorilla" and his "natural position was ON ALL FOURS."[10] Zip was William Henry Johnson of New Jersey and he had a strangely shaped head, but where the Wild Men of Borneo were fair complexioned, Johnson was black, and that agreed with the popular equating of dark skin with primitiveness.

Myths and Melanin

The origin of Western racial attitudes are too complex for this short history, but it includes the belief that nonwhites were created before Adam (Pre-Adamites) and a belief in polygenism, which is the separate creation of each race in ways suitable for their own part of the world. Perhaps the most influential idea, however, was the Great Chain of Being.

Beginning with Aristotle, and elaborated by classical, medieval, and Renaissance philosophers, the Great Chain of Being is a concept of the universe that dominated European and American thought until the eighteenth century and remained influential for considerably longer. The Great Chain of Being conceives of everything in the universe, both spiritual and material, as "linked" to the Creator through intermediate forms.

God is at the top of a *scala naturae* ("ladder" or "stairway of nature"), followed in descending order by angels, humans, animals, plants, the four elements, and minerals; dust or sand is at the bottom, and then nothingness. Every position is filled and every being's place in the hierarchy immutably fixed by its ratio of spirit to matter; more spirit means a higher position closer to God, with greater abilities and intelligence, and wielding authority over those beneath them. Large categories like humankind contain numerous subdivisions, so that kings and queens are superior to commoners, and the white race higher than blacks. Some argued that primitive groups like Bushmen, Hottentots (Khoikoin), and Australian Aboriginals were not even humble kinds of people, but higher forms of ape.

The persistence of these ideas is evident in books like Charles Carroll's *The Negro a Beast* (1900), in which Adam and Eve are progenitors of the white race "[i]n direct line of kinship with God" and scriptural arguments are used for expelling "the negro from his present unnatural position in the family of man, and the resumption of his proper place among the ape."[11] Like the Great Chain of Being, in which superiors rule over inferiors, the black man was "created with articulate speech and hands that he may be of service to his master—the White man," but Carroll does not rely solely on religion and brings in the findings of "race science."[12]

Anthropology, taxonomy, and other disciplines had devised human pecking orders based on different aspects of anatomy, especially "facial angles" (i.e., prognathism) and cranial capacity: calculating intelligence by the size and shape of brains (measuring heads was considered so important that museums acquired enormous collections of skulls). The dimensions of different races' skulls were tabulated, and researchers created painstakingly detailed charts showing the similarities between blacks and apes. Scientific racism, like racism based on religion, was used to justify slavery, colonialism, and antimiscegenation laws, with eugenicists decrying racial mixing and the resulting "feebleness and perishableness of the Mulatto."[13] The idea that blacks were somewhere between human and animal is reflected in the race of most sideshow wild men, but there were other desirable qualities such as ugliness (notoriously unattractive Brooklyn mobster Louis "Pretty" Amberg bragged about being offered a job as a wild man) or physical peculiarities like claws, fur, or horns, that could be portrayed as nonhuman.

The ideal candidate was probably black, ugly, a reasonably good performer, and a freak of nature, but if someone like that could not be found, they could be *made*.

Dentist and Doc

Much of this history takes place at, or around, the towns of Alma, Nicholls, and Waycross, Georgia. The area is north of Okefenokee Swamp, reputed home of several different monsters, including a thirteen-foot-tall "Man Mountain" who twisted the heads off five hunters before being gunned down in 1829, and "Pig Man," a local version of Florida's Skunk Ape; the eccentric wild men mentioned earlier are from all over the state, but whether these stories influenced Dr. Dedge, or his creation of the Okefenokee Wild Man, is unknown.[14]

The Dedge family came from France (D'Edge), and John R. Dedge was born at Baxley, Georgia, on March 11, 1865, one month before Lee surrendered at Appomattox. He married in 1886 and graduated from the Southern Medical College in 1890 as a doctor of dental surgery.

Standing six feet, one inch tall, with a thin face, high forehead, fair complexion, black hair, and dark eyes, Dedge was an imposing, even intimidating, figure and not just when striding toward patients with a pair of pliers. Even a longtime friend like George D. Lowe, Dedge's physician, did not trifle with the dentist. After Lowe advised him to live at a higher altitude,

> he solemnly petitioned the city fathers for permission to build a bungalow atop the city water tower and was very resentful when they turned him down. I thought it very funny and started to kid him about it, but he had a queer look in his eyes and I changed the subject.[15]

Nevertheless, he was as "good a dentist as ever drilled a cavity or crowned a tooth" and did other kinds of work, like vaccinating the employees of a lumber company.[16] Dr. Dedge also owned a plantation (most likely pine trees for collecting resin) and a turpentine "place" (probably for distilling the resin), but his main interest was money. The dentist was willing to counterfeit coins, smuggle diamonds, or go into show business if it meant turning a profit, and his friend William T. "Doc" Brinson was an experienced exhibitor.

At six feet, four inches tall and weighing somewhere between six hundred and seven hundred pounds, Brinson was even more impressive than Dedge. He rode about in a "buggy" that "resembles more nearly an army wagon," used "an enormous rocking chair, of cantilever construction, which has to be moved about with a derrick," and had reportedly done quite well displaying himself at fairs and sideshows as "the fattest man in the world."[17] There is no knowing who originated the idea of showing a wild man, but Brinson's experience and Dr. Dedge's expertise and ruthlessness augured well for the undertaking.

Dentists were often involved with wild man shows. They created protruding fangs for "amiable Negro boys from about the circus lot who are trained to growl, flash a set of fake tusks and eat raw meat . . . ," but the quality of the workmanship varied.[18] One nineteenth-century showman named Sam Ashbridge "had a good wild nigger, but his tusks didn't fit him, and he worried himself to death. You see, Sam wanted a novelty, and he had all the coon's teeth pulled. Then he got a set of false ones made—regular tusks, that came out over his lower lip. Why you never saw anything that looked more like a gorilla than that coon of Ashbridge's did. He only lived a season, though."[19] "Novelty" was essential to a good exhibit.

Dedge's partner in the venture, Charles J. Medders, was also an overseer on his plantation. Doc Brinson presumably took part, and there was J. C. English, but they needed one more; preferably someone not too bright and compliant enough to be the wild man.

"Zara, the Horned African Demon"

In August 1902, a reporter interviewed Mr. Calvin Bird, who had a strange story to tell. He said,

> "Dr. John Dada found me down in Central America and he brung me 'long back wif him to Pearson, Ga. I was borned in Natchez, Miss., but I was working down where Dr. John found me."[20]

Dedge pressured him into undergoing dental surgery, ostensibly to fix his teeth, and Bird, who had a superstitious awe of the dentist ("I tell you dat man got er powerful eye"), agreed. On Christmas Day, December 25, 1901, an operation transformed the reluctant patient into a "horned demon."

Bird's eyeteeth were removed and bridgework put into the openings—probably threaded gold crowns held in place with platinum posts extending into the root canal.[21] The crowns served as points of attachment for oversized fangs of some kind, possibly alligator teeth, which screwed on and protruded over his lips.[22]

Dedge shaved Bird's head, cut a rectangular flap into his scalp, and inserted a silver plate between the skin and bone. It was an H-shaped piece of metal, flat, but for a slight curve that allowed it to follow the dome of the skull, two to three inches long, and had two protruding threaded silver posts with eyelets. With that in place, the opening was sutured shut, except for the posts and eyelets, which were designed to protrude about half an inch through the skin. Bird woke to find "two little nubbins" on his head and, since he already considered the dentist a "hoodoo doctor," his first thought was "maybe Dr. John done conjured me inter de debbil an' den I'se skeerder dan ever."[23]

When the incisions healed, Dedge "killed many innocent goats before finding a pair of horns suiting his purpose" and attached them to the exposed posts so that they appeared to be growing from Bird's head.[24] Dedge now possessed "a freak that outclassed most museum attractions in the whole country," but there must have been rumors about what was happening, and the pair left town just before an "investigating committee" arrived.[25]

Calvin Bird was now "Zara, the demon," the "Wild African Wonder," and was displayed at North Carolina and Georgia until the tour was interrupted on March 15, 1902. "Zara" was arrested at Valdosta for firing a pistol in the street (he does not seem to have been wearing horns at the time). J. C. English was taken into custody and fined $52 for "exhibiting the negro, under charge of cheating and swindling."[26] Once their legal problems were settled, the show moved to Tennessee, where Dr. Dedge contracted with another exhibitor to show Bird up north. He went to Syracuse, New York, and was displayed at Kirk Park, which then had grandstands, stables, and fairgrounds.[27]

Bird recalled the spieler standing outside the canvas where he "would holler loud as he kin":

> "'Walk up, right dis way fer to see de greatest livin' curious thing in de hull world'—meanin' me back dar in de tent, an' I roll my eyes and look plumb hidgeous, I sure did.'"[28]

In addition to playing the wild man, however, he was expected to do manual labor, and after three months as "a wonder from Darkest Africa," Bird hung up his horns and quit.[29] Fearing that Dr. Dedge might track him down, he remained at Syracuse and eventually found his way to the Hospital of the Good Shepherd, where Dr. E. S. Van Duyn agreed to remove the plate; newspapers followed the progress of this unusual case.

On August 21, 1902, the operation began, but the anesthesia agitated Bird, who fought with attendants and, being "a big strong fellow," ran from the operating room and had to be carried back.[30] The surgery itself went smoothly, though the story has an odd postscript.

Calvin Bird was recovering on a cot in the ward with his head bandaged "in turban fashion," when a circus performer and equestrienne calling herself "Louisa Demate" appeared.[31]

She gave the newspapers a very different account of him, claiming that

> ten years ago, . . . this colored man saw a picture of a wild man with horns and became possessed of the idea of posing as "The Wild Man." He went to the managers of Barnum's Circus, for whom she was then working, she says, and asked to be made into such a freak as he had seen in the picture. By his request the operation was accordingly performed.

Miss Demate claims that the operation was performed by two Philadelphia surgeons, Drs. John Bunnell and Giles Crogdins. Bird was with Barnum for a time, and after that she left the show and lost all trace of him until she saw *The Post-Standard*'s account of the operations performed by Bird:

> Miss Demate visited Bird yesterday as he lay in his cot in a ward at the Hospital of the Good Shepherd. "Hello, Charlie, old boy," she said, for that was the name she said he used to go by.
>
> The man didn't recognize her until she told her name and where she had been, when he remembered her. The woman talked with Bird a few minutes and when she left promised to bring with her again some of his old acquaintances in the circus.[32]

Was Louisa Demate an old acquaintance, or was she there to intimidate Bird and divert attention from the story of "Dr. Dada"? Her account seems overrun with names and dates, and it would be interesting to know what she and the former wild man talked about. Even the promise to come back with "old acquaintances in the circus" might have been a veiled threat to return with Dr. Dedge, and, after Demate's appearance, Bird drops into obscurity.

"Meet Me at the Fair!"

The Louisiana Purchase Exposition, better known as the St. Louis World's Fair, was a massive display of new technologies and curiosities gathered from around the world that opened at St. Louis, Missouri, in 1904 (it is remembered today for the song in which the singer instructs a male friend to "Meet Me in St. Louis, Louis"). Among the attractions was a life-sized cast of a blue whale and, most famously, or infamously, the "Human Zoo," an ethnological display that allowed fairgoers to meet Apaches (including Geronimo), Igorots from the Philippines, and Congolese pygmies. St. Louis was the ideal venue for Dr. Dedge's wild man show, so he found a young man named Perry Werks (or Weeks) to take Bird's place.

Werks shined shoes at Nicholls and agreed to have the

necessary hardware installed in his head for $50.[33] A description of how it was done appears as an amusing anecdote in the *Illinois Medical Journal* and, though the author does not claim to have firsthand knowledge, the description suggests that Dedge experimented with different ways of attaching horns. In Werks's case,

> [a]n incision was made over the vertex from one ear to the other, and a silver plate was introduced under the scalp about five inches long, in which there was a female screw, and then in the deer's horn the male screw was inserted. When it was entirely healed a minute puncture was made for the projecting male screw, and no one could discover that the horns had not actually grown in that place.[34]

When the showmen arrived in Missouri, they were not allowed on the fairgrounds but spent several profitable weeks as part of a carnival company, entertaining some of the exposition's twenty million visitors.[35]

Confusion apparently arose between Dedge's alligator-fanged wild man, now advertised as being from South Africa, and the single most popular figure at the fair, a Mbuti pygmy named Ota Benga, whose teeth were sharpened to dagger points. (Ota Benga later lived at New York City's Bronx Zoo and was exhibited in the monkey house with the orangutan, a juxtaposition between "low man" and "high ape" that points to the Great Chain of Being's influence on race science.) The idea that Dedge's wild man was "[a] featured attraction at the Louisiana Purchase Exposition" added to the show's appeal, and it made so much money that Werks "was about to skip and join another show which promised a higher salary, when his Waycross managers decided to saw off his horns thereby ruining his chances for exhibiting as a freak."[36]

If this story is true, Dedge must have changed his mind, since Werks returned to Georgia and continued to perform

> in a steel cage and fed a diet of raw meat and some whiskey. When he let out a blood curdling growl and with the blood from the raw meat running out of the corner of his mouth, even the bravest did not care to tarry too long in his presence.[37]

At Valdosta, police raided the show, but Werks managed to slip away, escaping to Doc Brinson's house at Waycross. Perry's sister-in-law, Alalee Werks, "who lived in the Bolen Community in 1964, said Perry died in Waycross, Georgia about 1937 and was buried in the cemetery at Nicholls, Georgia."[38]

After their St. Louis success, the partners talked about going to Coney Island; they just needed another wild man.[39]

Horns and Coins

The next to wear the horns was George Brown. Nothing is known about him before November 1905, when Brown applied to Dr. Walter Ryan of Springfield, Illinois, for help.

He told the doctor that a year and a half earlier, a plate was inserted in his head for holding goat horns, and since then he had been exhibited across Georgia as a wild man. There is no mention of Coney Island, or how Brown got to Illinois, but the plate had slipped and was causing him considerable discomfort.

Ryan assumed that the man was joking or crazy until he inspected Brown's scalp and found the points. Neither the doctor nor anyone else outside the Hospital of the Good Shepherd at Syracuse had seen anything like it before, and when Dr. Ryan removed the plate at St. John's Hospital, a number of local physicians watched the procedure. (Dedge's work always drew a crowd. He later told George Lowe that everything had been going well until they "struck Evanston, Illinois, where the Humane Society raised a row and made him dehorn his money maker."[40] Springfield is two hundred miles from Evanston, and Dedge does not say when he had problems with the Humane Society, so connecting the two incidents is guesswork.) Meanwhile, the business partners returned to Georgia, having reportedly earned a fortune, and took a long holiday; perhaps Dedge decided to retire from show business altogether.

The next five years were presumably spent pulling teeth and distilling turpentine, but the calm was broken in February 1910, when U.S. Secret Service men arrested Dr. Dedge for being part of a counterfeiting ring.[41]

They discovered a box in his overcoat pocket containing fake $10 gold pieces, "apparently made of a white metal plated with gold," the workmanship of which was "pronounced by the officers as about the best they ever saw."[42] The package arrived by mail, so when the case came before a grand jury the wily dentist claimed to believe that it contained "dental supplies which he had ordered, and that he did not know who sent him the spurious coins, or where they came from."[43] It sounded reasonable to the jury and Dedge was turned loose to begin work on his fourth exhibit.

Last of the Wild Men

Joe Wright's account of his time as a wild man is the most complete and problematic.

It began in the now-familiar way, with a black man, Wright, arriving at the County Hospital of Thomasville, Georgia, with an unusual problem. The silver plate in his head had shifted, causing an infection, and he asked Dr. Arthur D. Little to take it out. His explanation for how the plate got there, however, was bizarre.

Several months earlier, four white men came to his house

one night and, surrounding him with guns pointed, ordered him to come with them. Under the circumstances he naturally went, and was taken to the office of the doctor, where something was given him to put him to sleep.[44]

When he woke up, the knobs were sticking through his head and Dr. Dedge explained that they were for attaching goat horns.

Joe says that it gave him great pain, and after some time he managed to escape from the room where he was confined and made his way to a doctor, who took off the knobs but left the silver plate next to the skull. This he found very uncomfortable, and so he came to Dr. Little, the county physician, to have it removed, it not being his ambition to figure as a "horned man"; it looks as if he was in a fair way to be exhibited as a curiosity but for his timely escape.[45]

This story appeared in the newspaper on March 6. By the seventh, Wright's account had changed, saying that he had actually spent years in Dedge's employ working as a wild man. Dr. Little later published an article based on the revised version of the story titled "The Goat Man."

He writes that the twenty-three-year-old Wright "had an acute attack of wanderlust"[46] and got a job on a steamer, but the combination of hard labor and seasickness proved too much, and he was dropped off at an unnamed port. There,

> [h]e found that he could hardly understand the language of his newly found people nor could he be understood,

> but finally some one met him and said, "Hello nigger." He recognized an American white gentleman, who was later to play an important role in his life. Expressing much joy at seeing some one who could understand him, he followed his friend on a fruit steamer to South America, informing his newly found white man that he was henceforth his negro and faithful servant.[47]

Dr. Little's article provides the most detailed description of how the plates and fangs were made. The dentist

> hammered out an H-shaped plate from South American silver coin and, brazing on to it two threaded knobs, proposed to embed it beneath the scalp of his servant and put taps of magnificent goat horns in the butt ends so that the horns could be screwed on and off at will. He further proposed to put Logan crowns [posts going into the root canal with attached crowns] on his servant's eye teeth and in this way attach two vicious tusks of the wild boar. These, likewise in a way that could be removed at will.[48]

The operation was performed at a log cabin on the banks "of a certain river" (probably at Pearson, Georgia) and, after Wright recovered and learned how to be a wild man, they began traveling from town to town. "Money came easy," particularly after joining an unnamed "exposition," and everything was going well until

> [o]ne night, after closing, as the owner was sweetly dreaming of yachts and palaces, it occurred to the trainer that his wild man needed a little sight-seeing and refreshments. So, suiting the action to thought, he proceeded to administer spiritus frumenti to his man and himself, when lo and behold! his wild man became unmanageable [and] was causing a riot. The police interfered, and looking for the easiest point to control the goat man, a cop grabbed a horn and, who are we petty mortals to criticize the creator of this wonderful being that his horns were not made for rough handling, the horn came away revealing the metal tap in the butt . . . as soon as the owner heard that all was discovered he immediately gave bond for the new [*sic*] useless [exhibit] and both left the city post-haste.[49]

After leaving the sideshow, Wright worked at a sawmill, but the knobs "caused headache when overheated by the Southern sun." He asked a blacksmith for help and, "laying his head near the anvil with the knobs lying thereon, the valiant blacksmith proceeded to trim the knobs to less inconvenient length."[50] This rough work caused a suppurative infection to set in, and "[p]us was easily pressed from around the knobs," which brought Wright to the hospital.[51]

Dr. Little cut through the scars and, "with patience and perseverance," removed the silver plate intact. It was later stolen from his office, but skeptics were told that there were "witnesses to the operation and many people who saw the plate."

Though the article was published twenty years after the event, there is no reason for thinking it is inaccurate as far as the doctor's actions or his recounting of Wright's narrative are concerned. The latter's reliability is another question.

His initial claim of being abducted and forced to undergo surgery recalls black folklore about "night doctors," physicians who kidnapped black people for experiments and dissection (in fact, slaves were used for medical research, and black burial grounds were plundered relentlessly to supply anatomy classes). Beyond that, the story that Wright told Dr. Little might have been assembled from a scrapbook of other wild men's experiences; he was displayed at an exposition like Perry Werks, he met Dr. Dedge by accident in Central or South America the way Calvin Bird did, and his arrest is a retelling of Bird's run-in with the police. The story seems unlikely, but it does highlight the exhibit's history of problems with the law, particularly at Valdosta, which raises another question: Why was it raided?

Police are traditionally suspicious of traveling shows and their attendant con men, gamblers, and pickpockets, but chief of police Calvin Dampier might have been warier than most. In 1902, the year Bird drunkenly fired a gun in the street, an elephant with the Harris Nickel-Plate Circus trampled its trainer to death, ran through Valdosta, then wandered into the countryside, where Chief Dampier shot it with a borrowed Mauser. Nevertheless, the raid that ended Perry Werks's association with the show is never explained. The word suggests a more organized police operation and raises the possibility that Dr. Dedge was using the exhibit as a cover for "shoving the queer," that is, putting counterfeit money into circulation.

Whatever the truth, his career as an exhibitor might have ended with Joe Wright's departure, but the dentist's enthusiasm for making money and indifference toward the law remained undiminished.

Murder on Main Street

John Dedge and his longtime business partner Charles J. Medders had a falling-out around 1919, possibly over a plan to smuggle diamonds into the United States by sewing them inside dog hides.[52] They parted company and the sixty-three-year-old Medders became a justice of the peace, opened a law office, and bought a small grocery store on Main Street (now 11th) at Alma; Dr. Dedge, however, was not satisfied. He reportedly "considered you either with him or against him" and his former associate might have known too much about various enterprises for the dentist's peace of mind.

On the night of July 10, 1920, Medders was locking up his store on Main Street when a shotgun boomed from a parked Liberty 6 coupe and "[n]ine buckshot entered his head and neck, killing him outright."[53] The assassin's automobile was traced back to Dr. Dedge, who was arrested with two accomplices.

Over the next ten months, Dedge was tried for murder three times before being convicted and sentenced to life in prison. The sheriff denied rumors about special treatment, but "[t]here are those . . . who claimed that Dr. Dedge did install his equipment in the County jail and continued extracting and filling teeth."[54] He served three years and was released.

Dedge's friend W. T. "Doc" Brinson died of apoplexy at age sixty-four on August 4, 1926. Doc was put in an oversized coffin and ten pallbearers carried him to his grave at the Lott Cemetery at Waycross. John Dedge followed two weeks later; the sixty-one-year-old dentist-showman-murderer died on August 16, 1926, and is buried in the Rose Hill Cemetery at Alma.[55]

That means he was gone nine or ten years when young Braswell Deen's boss said, "There goes Dr. Dedge and his wild man"; but perhaps he said, "There goes Dr. Dedge's wild man."

Wild at Alma

There were four Okeefenokee Wild Men, though none were apparently advertised as such. Three had the plates removed and gave accounts of themselves that were unusual enough to be printed in newspapers, along with the names of the patients, doctors, and hospitals where the surgery was performed. The sole exception is Perry Werks. Apart from a threat to cut off his horns at St. Louis, there is nothing to suggest that the hardware was ever removed; furthermore, he lived at Waycross, just twenty-five miles from Alma, and is not excluded by age.

Werks was a young man when Dr. Dedge hired him. If he was twenty years old in 1904, then he would have been around fifty in the mid-1930s—on the old side, perhaps, for the knockabout life of a touring sideshow performer, but it was the Great Depression, when poverty and unemployment could have forced the most reluctant wild man out of retirement.

Judge Deen found an old drawing of the horned man and writes that the wild man "[l]ooked like the image . . . [with] old clothes, horns, but [I] did not see any alligator teeth."[56] The horns in the picture seem too far apart to have been supported by Bird's plate, which was no more than three inches long, or Werks's, which was five inches (assuming the *Illinois Medical Journal* is correct). His identity may never be known for certain, but among Dr. Dedge's wild men, Perry Werks remains the likeliest candidate.

Swamp Satyr

Even a modest sideshow attraction must excite some degree of awe, fear, or wonder; the Okefenokee Wild Man did that, while confirming popular prejudices.

During slavery, blacks were portrayed as "docile, childlike people who required the care and guidance of paternalistic whites."[57] By the late 1880s, a generation after the Emancipation Proclamation, a new myth appeared about black men, in which they were seen as rapists preying on white women. It became one of the most pernicious aspects of racism, especially in the South, where the horrors of lynching were justified as an effective form of deterrence. ("When these black fiends keep their hands off the throats of the women of the South," said Congressman Thomas Upton Sisson of Mississippi, "then lynching will stop . . ."[58]) Many came to believe that "any black man was a potential rapist for all blacks were susceptible to attacks of 'sexual madness' which compelled them to rape white women."[59] When Dr. Dedge attached sharp, piercing, "masculine and phallic" horns to representatives of "primitive masculinity in its purest, most primal form," he took the concept of black man as hypersexual brute and realized it in the form of an American satyr.[60]

Like its classical forebears, the Okeefenokee Wild Man embodied "untamed nature, licence, and lust"; by caging it and charging a nickel admission, the showman made it possible for audiences to see their fantasies about race and sex brought to life, and emerge from the experience unscathed.[61]

The exhibit's popularity speaks to people's continuing fascination with wild men and, sixty years after seeing one himself, Braswell Deen Jr. rendered the experience in verse. He used the wild man as a symbol, but instead of brutality, the wilderness, or some other traditional meaning, it represents fraud.

Piltdown (Wild) Man?

A wild man on the streets of Alma was not the most dramatic event in Judge Deen's life. As a Marine during World War II, he took part in the invasions of Peleliu and Okinawa, and was wounded in combat. Appointed to the Georgia Court of Appeals in 1965, he spent twenty-five years on the bench, two as chief judge, and retired in 1990. Since then the "Christian, Constitution, Conservative, US Marine, Lawyer, Legislator, Judge, Arbitrator, Mediator, Author & Composer!" has directed his energies toward defending and supporting the biblical account of Creation.[62]

Judge Deen's books, essays, and poems include the eighty-two-line "Wild Man of the Okeefenokee!," which describes how Dr. Dedge created his exhibit by attaching goat horns to a "low-browed Black Man" and putting "him in a cage with bars, pulled by his car while adorned." Then

Dr. Dedge with His Good Friend Caged, the "Wild Man of Okefenokee"
Toured America as a museum attraction. They collected, much money.
Purporting to be Evolution's Exhibit A of half man and half beast,
Many who paid to view the freak, thought it weird, but also funny.

Calling the Okeefenokee Wild Man "Evolution's Exhibit A" was ballyhoo, of course, and no more serious than Barnum declaring Zip the missing link, but the judge uses it as a point of departure for exploring dubious episodes in the history of Darwinism. These include the Piltdown Man hoax, a fossilized peccary tooth once identified as belonging to a primitive human ("Nebraska Man"), and the disappearance of allegedly convincing evidence such as the fossils of Java Man. Judge Deen suggests that the foundations of evolution are shaky and compares those espousing it to

A grocery man, selling underweight butter, or, using their false scales,
Or, advertising adulterated foodstuffs . . .

Rather than science, it as an ideology, and textbooks biased

Where, only data supposedly supporting the sacred cow of evolution
Appears; non-ape ancestry notions, are disallowed.

This leads him to conclude that

Thus, goes the, true story, of this, "The Wild Man of Okefenokee!"
And, another example, of hot air evolution, hokum, for all to see![63]

Holy Geist

A visitor passing through the small historic district of Middleway, West Virginia, might wonder why so many signs are decorated with scissors and crescents. There is a reason for these curious ornaments, which recall a time in the village's history when something invisible was starting fires, galloping like a horse, and relentlessly snipping away at boots and breeches. They called it the "Livingston Wizard" or "Wizard Clip," a name that came to be applied to Middleway itself (along with "Cliptown" or "Clip"), whose residents became known as "Clippers" and that was, in all probability, the only community in the United States ever named after a poltergeist.

The name "Livingston Wizard" comes from the family that was the main object of its attention and whose prolonged contact with the paranormal went beyond the usual noise and destruction of poltergeists, that it raises questions about how the phenomenon is perceived and even used.

In the eighteenth century, when Middleway was called Smithfield and West Virginia was part of the Virginia colony, a German immigrant named Johann Georg Liebenstein owned a large property adjacent to the settlement. Liebenstein lived in Pennsylvania, where he settled after fleeing the religious conflicts and oppressive taxes of the German Palatinate in 1723, and raised a family.[1] His son Adam (originally John Adam), the first of eleven surviving children, was born on February 16, 1739.

Adam attended a school operated by the Christ Evangelical Lutheran Church in nearby York, learned farming and his father's trade of linen weaving. He married, had a family, and, as the eldest son, inherited the largest portion of Johann's estate in 1771. It included a loom and the 350 acres next to Smithfield, Virginia.

At some point, their name was anglicized to *Livingston* and they headed south. It is unclear who made the trip, or when, and the family suffered a series of disasters.[2] The cattle died and the barn burned down, but whether this happened before or after the move to Virginia is unclear. They might have left sometime during 1771–1772, or as late as the 1790s, but historians agree that by the 1790s, the family was living outside Smithfield.

Little is known about Adam Livingston himself. He was

Pennsylvania Dutch; spoke more German than English; and the neighbors considered him respectable, honest, and industrious. He was around fifty years old when the troubles began, and his youngest child was nearly twenty.

The Wizard Clips

There are many accounts of the events that would afflict and enlighten the family, but only two are by people who knew the principals or witnessed phenomena: Mrs. Anastasia McSherry, a devoutly Roman Catholic neighbor, and Father Demetrius Augustine Gallitzin, a Russian prince and "the Apostle of the Alleghenies."[3] They heard phantom hooves inside the Livingstons' house and described the disappearance of money, stones moving across the floor by "invisible hands," beds bursting into flame, and "strange noises [that] terrified them at night."[4] Other sources describe crockery thrown on the floor, livestock dying, and spontaneous decapitation of poultry, but the "regular and most frequent *preternatural fact*" was the cutting up of everything made from cloth and leather.[5] Items laid out for washing, stored inside drawers, or even on the wearer's back were likely to be destroyed.

Father Gallitzin told a story about an "old Presbyterian lady" who heard about the clipping and visited the Livingston home:

> However, before entering, she took her new black silk cap off her head, wrapped it up in her silk handkerchief, and put it in her pocket, to save it from being *clipt*. After a while, she stept out again, to go to home, and having drawn the handkerchief out of her pocket and opened it, she found her cap cut up into narrow ribbons.[6]

Some reports describe the sound of scissors at work and, since the fabric was cut and not torn, the phenomenon became known as "Wizard Clip." Clothing was found riddled with crescent-shaped holes done "exactly with the thread, as if a tailor had done it," while footwear was spiral-sliced, so that a boot that appeared to be whole collapsed into one long leather string. This went on for a long time—possibly years—before Livingston sought help.[7]

He approached his minister, the Rev. Christian Streit, explained what was happening, and begged for assistance, pointing out that Christ's disciples were given authority to cast out unclean spirits. Streit allegedly replied that "that power existed only in olden times, but was done away now," so he could not help.[8] An Episcopalian minister tried exorcising the Wizard but was "famously abused by the spirit" and his prayer book deposited in a chamber pot, while a Methodist retreated before a shower of stones.

Livingston also tried magic. The Pennsylvania Dutch have a traditional form of magic called powwowing or *braucherie*, and cunning men suggested herbs, the *Book of*

Common Prayer, and a "riddle, by way of catching the Devil"; these also ended up in the chamber pot.[9] Three men from Winchester also attempted to drive out the devil (who is not mentioned), but a large stone came out of the fireplace and whirled around on the floor for fifteen minutes, and they left.

It was an Irish peddler who spent a sleepless night listening to the Wizard racketing around the Livingstons' house, advised sending for a Roman Catholic priest, but Adam "answered quickly that he had tried so many of these fellows that he was not going to try any more of them."[10] Whether this response was borne out of general disgust with clergymen or Lutheran suspicions about the Catholic Church, the Wizard kept clipping and Livingston finally relented.

Priests were rare in eighteenth-century Virginia and explanations for how Adam finally met one vary, but in the end, Father Dennis Cahill; Mrs. McSherry's husband, Richard; and a man named Minghini gathered at Livingston's farmhouse.[11] Father Cahill was skeptical. He thought neighbors were playing tricks and hurried through the prayers, sprinkled some holy water, and was on his way out when "a sum of money which had disappeared from out of the old man's chest was by invisible hands laid on the door sill, between the priest's feet."[12]

These ministrations brought the Livingstons some peace, but it was not long before the poltergeist returned and Father Gallitzin attempted an exorcism. As he began, "the rattling and rumbling as of innumerable wagons . . . filled the house," causing the young priest to lose his nerve, so the more "truculent" Father Cahill was summoned, and he expelled the Wizard forever.[13] Livingston was so grateful that the family converted to Roman Catholicism, but a cessation of clipping did not mean that life would return to normal.

A blinding light began to fill their house at night, accompanied by a mysterious voice that instructed the family in the Roman Catholic faith.

The Voice Speaks

The source of the Voice was invisible to all but young children, though Adam sometimes saw the sign of the cross being made by a phantom hand and arm that physically struck him when he tried grabbing them.[14] There is no description of how the Voice sounded, but it sang beautifully in Latin and English and must have spoken German as well to communicate with the Livingstons. Most assumed it was the spirit of a priest, and the Voice did claim that it had once been alive and said Livingston would learn its identity before he died.

It never taught unorthodox doctrines but emphasized the power of the Blessed Virgin and the special importance of praying for those who suffered in Purgatory. When the Voice became the Livingstons' spiritual director, these souls played an important part in their lives, with their screams overwhelming Adam as he worked in the field and waking the family at night.[15] The Voice demanded that they spend hours in prayer to alleviate the souls' suffering, demonstrating the pain they endured by burning a handprint into a cloth; it also seared the first three letters of Jesus's name, *IHS*, in a waistcoat.[16] The Voice was not given to subtle lessons. It warned the McSherrys' daughters against vanity by shattering a mirror and illustrated the danger of last-minute repentance by making a priest's horse invisible so he could not find it, thus preventing him from reaching a dying woman in time to give her absolution.

In addition to the Voice, a second spiritual teacher visited the Livingstons in the form of a bearded old man. He was ragged and barefoot, but when Adam offered him a pair of shoes, the stranger replied that they were not needed where he came from. The "Angel" spent several days instructing the family in Catholicism, telling them that Luther and Calvin are in hell suffering increased tortures every time their teachings cause another soul to be damned. The old man finally walked through the front gate and vanished.[17]

Despite a parade of wonders, Mrs. Livingston remained the self-described "Judas" of the family. Her conversion was not sincere and she challenged the Voice in different ways, such as her attempt to serve meat soup on a Friday. She locked a bowl of it in the cellar and later discovered the soup gone, replaced by an equal amount of clean water. In addition to changing or transporting foodstuffs, the Voice interpreted dreams, saw events happening at a distance, and foretold the future, including Mrs. Livingston's death. It said she would die at home and open her eyes in hell if she did not submit to the rules of the Roman Catholic Church, and though its harassment often drove her to stay with neighbors, this prediction, like others, proved accurate.

When the cradle containing Mrs. McSherry's infant son was violently rocked by invisible hands, the Voice told her, through Livingston, that the devil wanted to destroy the infant who would be his enemy; William McSherry grew up to be a Jesuit priest. In 1802, Livingston deeded thirty-five acres of land to the church, and the Voice declared that "[b]efore the end of time [it] would be a great place of prayer and fasting and praise!"[18]

Many believed the area was haunted and avoided it, but some local Catholics considered the land sanctified by miracles and used it as a burial ground. Two of Livingston's oldest children and/or his two wives were already interred there, as well as an "Unknown Stranger" who is the subject of the best-known legend about the Wizard Clip.

According to the story, a man appeared at the Livingston home and was invited to spend the night. He became ill and begged for a priest, but Adam said that he did not know any, and if he did, he would not allow one in his house, so the stranger died without making his final confession; their troubles began soon after. This story first appeared in 1883 and though it is almost certainly an invention, a stranger *is* buried on Livingston's property in a grave that is marked by a large freestanding cross inscribed "In Memory of the Unknown Stranger 1797," which reminds people to pray for all souls. (When the author visited in July 2007, there were rosaries wrapped around the cross.)

In 1809, Livingston sold the farm and moved to Greenfield Township, Pennsylvania. Father Gallitzin lived twenty miles away in Loretto and often celebrated Mass at the old man's home. There is no record of paranormal phenomena at the new location, and if the Voice revealed its identity to Livingston before his death in 1820, he kept the knowledge to himself.

As for the land, questions about its ownership were not resolved until 1922, when the Richmond Court confirmed that it belonged to the church. A small All Souls' Chapel was built in 1923 and the place was largely forgotten until 1978, when construction began on the new pastoral center at what became known as "Priest Field."

The Wizard's Voice

Working on the assumption that the accounts are more or less true, the Livingstons appear to have experienced a poltergeist outbreak followed by a long-term haunting.

Those involved and their contemporaries presumably

held the traditional view that poltergeists are caused by black magic, and dubbed it the Wizard Clip or the Livingston Wizard. Unlike other notorious cases, however, like the Drummer of Tedworth or Tennessee's Bell Witch, no one was accused of witchcraft or suspected of bearing the family a grudge. Mrs. Mary Ann Taylor's mother (born 1782) told a story in which the Wizard was the spirit of a man who committed murder to obtain the land later occupied by Livingston, while later versions portray the Wizard as the aggrieved spirit of a stranger.[19] The various explanations reflect different folk beliefs and perhaps the influence of nineteenth-century Spiritualism; by the twentieth century, explanations for the poltergeist had shifted almost exclusively to living "agents." These are individuals, or groups, that create poltergeist phenomena through unconscious psychokinesis, which is why poltergeist outbreaks are sometimes described as "haunted people" rather than haunted houses.[20]

Whatever caused the manifestations, the idea of the Wizard and the Voice as separate entities might be less useful than thinking of them as different phases of the same phenomenon. This idea is supported by a letter from Mrs. Livingston that appeared in the September 12, 1798, issue of the *Potomak Guardian*, in which she states that "the trouble still remains in the Livingston's family, at times, in a greater or lesser degree, in spite of *Priestly art*."[21] The letter (presumably written with help) goes on to say that clergymen and spirits were separating her from her husband and family and trying to take her land, which could not be sold or donated without the wife's consent.[22] This is the only surviving statement by someone intimately involved, but not a pious Catholic, and suggests a very different interpretation of events.

It is a reminder that the Voice's actions—if not its motives—were often indistinguishable from the Wizard's; they both terrified members of the family, kept everyone awake, and stole or destroyed valuable objects. Why, for example, did the Voice take a piece of linen, keep it three weeks, and leave it folded on a bush? What if the Voice was responsible for the screaming that was supposed to come from souls in Purgatory? And did it shake Michael McSherry's cradle and blame the devil?

Roman Catholic writers have considered this question and point to the results. The Voice taught orthodox doctrines and brought about more than fourteen conversions, while the successful exorcism of the Wizard Clip confirmed the Catholic priest's status as a true disciple of Christ. Mrs. Livingston's letter, however, is not the only dissenting view.

Adam and his children Henry and Eve did become devout, but a nonbeliever might wonder about his wife being driven from home, along with the six other children; according to Father Gallitzin they were "scattered away, and I believe care very little for the Church."[23] As for the physical evidence, that has been lost.

Some of the Wizard/Voice's handiwork was given to a

mission house at Conewago, Pennsylvania, including dresses "cut in small half moons, in straight rows, as tho' machinery—cut close together—without even space that one button could cover left—cut, all over." Another source describes "semi-circular figures an inch or two long."[24] (How it did the cutting is another mystery. Despite the snipping sounds, there is no evidence that the Wizard Clip used ordinary tools, but along with the Voice, it did set fires, produce blinding light, and scorch recognizable designs into cloth. Perhaps the cutting was done with heat like a modern laser cutter. They work quickly and leave a finished, slightly singed edge, and any odor that might result would go unnoticed in smoky eighteenth-century interiors.) Father Matthew Leken destroyed the Conewago collection in 1830, while the vest marked *IHS* was given to the Sisters of the Visitation in Kaskaskia, Illinois, and survived until 1844, when it was lost in a flood.

The Livingstons' home, the "haunted house," was in ruins by 1864 and has long since disappeared, along with the original chapel. It is now the Priest Field Pastoral Center, a small complex of modern buildings and gardens open to all Christian denominations (a concession the Voice would *not* have approved). There is a new All Souls' Chapel and a path through the forest that leads to the Unknown Stranger's grave; at the trailhead stands a rugged wooden relief carving of Adam Livingston facing a fiery cross and trampling crescents underfoot.

The last known claim of clipping was made by two young men who said that dollar bills in their wallets had been cut into half moons, but the staff believes it was a hoax and that they were connected to anti-Catholic literature found in the woods. There are vague stories about glasses or camera straps being destroyed, but strange phenomena apparently ceased long ago. It is almost two hundred years since the Wizard clipped or the Voice spoke at Priest Field, which is a peaceful place where one hears little more than bird calls, wind chimes, and the distant splashing of Opequon Creek.

The Man in Room 41 and Other Autodecapitants

> **Self-decapitation is an extremely difficult, not to say dangerous, thing to attempt . . .**
>
> —W. S. Gilbert, *The Mikado*

Living in a downstairs apartment means getting used to unidentified noises overhead. A thump could be anything from an overweight tabby jumping off the sofa to the lady upstairs being attacked by a razor-wielding orangutan. If guests had been staying in the room directly below room 41 at the Lahr House hotel at Lafayette, Indiana, on the morning of Sunday, June 11, 1876, they might have heard the sound of a single muted crack come through the ceiling at around seven A.M. and, unless they also happened to have imaginations of almost exquisite morbidity, are unlikely to have guessed that it was the sound of a man beheading himself in a way journalists of the period could only describe as "The Most Wonderful Suicide in the History of the World."

Headlessness: How Some People Get That Way

Deliberate self-decapitation is rare, but there are a number of ways the head and body can become separated in the course of conventional suicides. A shotgun fired at close range can sever the neck, and explosives, of course, can blow the body apart; in 1951 an elderly farmer in Wausau, Wisconsin, detonated a stick of dynamite under his chin and was beheaded.[1] In rare cases, decapitation can occur as a result of hanging, particularly if the person is heavy, the drop too long, or the line too thin or inelastic. It has even occurred during lawful executions.

When "Black Jack" Ketchum was hanged at Clayton, New Mexico, in 1901, "the half-inch rope severed his head as cleanly as if a knife had cut it." To make matters worse, the "headless trunk" then "pitched forward toward the spectators and blood spurted upon those nearest the scaffold."[2] Even suicide by cutting the throat can result in beheading.

Around the time of Ketchum's death, a headless body was found near Edgemont Park in East St. Louis, Illinois. A month later, in May 1901, the head was found a hundred yards away, wrapped in an old coat and with a rusty razor nearby. The coroner's jury decided that it was suicide, which meant that when the unidentified man cut his throat, the blade passed through the cervical vertebrae (how the body came to be three hundred feet from the razor and head is another question). Some have wondered whether self-decapitation with an edged tool or weapon is possible, yet there are other examples; self-beheading with obsidian knives may have even been a part of Mayan religious rituals, which brings us to the rare cases of suicide by deliberate self-beheading or, to coin a word, "autodecapitation."

They account for less than one in a hundred suicides and typically involve a male placing his neck on railroad tracks and waiting for the train.[3] In another form of "vehicle-assisted decapitation," one end of a rope is tied to a stationary object like a tree, and the other to the neck of the person committing suicide; he or she then drives away till the rope yanks the head off (for some reason, this has been done by a number of husbands angry at their wives).[4] It resembles decapitation by hanging, but with the headless body seated at the wheel of a moving vehicle. Chainsaws and cutting machines are also employed. Mrs. Fred Sheets of Hinton, Oklahoma, in a rare example of female self-beheading, died in her husband's butcher shop when, "in a fit of despondency . . . [she] laid her head on an automatic electric cheese slicer and severed it."[5]

All of these cases involve the application of conventional

objects and devices to decapitation; instruments created for the specific purpose of suicidal beheading are rare. One example reportedly existed in India:

> It was half-moon shaped, with a sharp edge, was fastened at the back of the neck, chains being attached to the ends. The man who donned this instrument of death put his feet in the chains, gave a sharp jerk downward and severed his head from the body.[6]

As an American and a child of the Industrial Revolution, James Moon thought in terms of mechanical, not muscular, power and used it, along with the power of modern communications, to realize his ambitions.

Mr. Moon's Busy Day and Night

In 1876, Moon was a thirty-seven-year-old farmer, blacksmith, Union Army veteran, and inventor who lived with his wife, Mary, and their six children on a farm at Farmer's Institute, a Quaker community nine miles south of Lafayette. He taught himself blacksmithing and was an inventor interested, like many of his contemporaries, in perpetual motion, and in perfecting the sewing machine; Moon was temperate and spent his leisure time carving items out of wood with a penknife.

His father, Enoch Moon, was a minister in the Society of Friends, and James "could quote the Bible from beginning to end," but he was also a skeptic about religion and, contrary to Quaker teachings, served in the army; the relationship between father and son was strained. Neighbors apparently regarded James Moon as unreliable, but his home life was happy and, on the evening of Friday, June 9, his wife, Mary, could not help noticing that her normally pleasant and genial husband was in particularly good spirits.

The next morning, Moon harnessed the horse to the wagon. He was a big man, with brown hair and eyes, who stood six feet, two inches and weighed 190 pounds, yet he might have needed his son's assistance in getting a heavy trunk onto the wagon bed. When it was loaded he left for Lafayette, arriving around ten A.M. Moon tied up the horse and went into Lahr House, a landmark hotel on Main Street, to rent a "good" room for three or four days. He said he was a light sleeper who needed someplace quiet, so Moon looked at several rooms before deciding that number 41 suited him "first rate."[7] It was on the third floor at the rear of the building and he had reportedly stayed in the same room three years earlier. Moon then left to run errands.

His exact itinerary is unknown, but he bought the head of an ax with a broad, 12-inch cutting edge at Beach's hardware store and carried it to Harding & Son's foundry. There, Moon bought two pieces of thick iron plate from the foundry's stock and instructed the clerk to bore holes through the plates and ax head, then bolt the three pieces together into a single unit. He explained that it was going to be part of a machine he was inventing for making fruit baskets. Like most farmers at the time, Moon had a full beard, so while the ironwork was being done he found a barbershop, emerging clean-shaven and redolent of witch hazel and bay rum.

At R. Schwegler & Brother's drugstore, Moon bought cotton batting and a bottle containing two or three ounces of chloroform, then picked up the modified ax head (which now weighed between forty and sixty pounds), returned to his wagon, and put it inside the trunk. Two porters then wrestled the trunk and its contents up to the hotel room, with Moon making sure the box was kept upright and not dropped, for the contents "would not permit jostling."[8] He told the Lahr's manager, Otho T. Weakley, that he "was engaged in perfecting a patent of considerable importance,"[9] and, with the trunk in the room and everything arranged satisfactorily, Moon locked the door and left again.

He met some friends and was "cheerful, laughing and talking familiarly and freely with his acquaintances, giving special attention to army reminiscences."[10] Moon presumably ate dinner, and climbed the stairs to his room between eight and nine o'clock. He had a long night ahead, for he was preparing to introduce his invention to the world in a way that would give even the most ruthless publicist pause.

Moon went to his room but did not retire. The noise of

hammering and pounding coming from number 41 grew so loud that other guests complained and Mr. Weakley went up to ask if he was rebuilding the room; Moon replied that he was working on an important invention and would pay for any damages. This episode might be a later addition, since the machine was held together with screws and bolts so "there would be no noise necessary in erecting it" and the only tools in Moon's trunk were a wrench, a screwdriver, and a brace with three bits.[11] Whatever the truth, the third floor was quiet by midnight and the other inmates of Lahr House went to sleep.

Sunday, June 11, proved to be oppressively hot. Temperatures made "shirt bosoms melt like butter," and by five P.M., Lahr chambermaid Bridget Clogan's patience was exhausted.[12] She had to clean number 41, and after knocking all day without response, the sixteen-year-old Clogan went into the adjoining room, number 40, where she used a passkey to unlock the communicating door.

Her first thought might have been surprise at the presence of a large wood and metal beam in the hotel room, but any curiosity about it ended with the sight of the bloody corpse. Clogan's screams echoed down the passage, summoning two men, Mr. Tinney of Lafayette and Mr. Lance, a traveling salesman from Cincinnati, who took in the grisly scene; they sent for the hotel clerks, who then summoned authorities.

Third-Class Lever, First-Class Beheading

"And then I fell suddenly calm, and lay smiling at the glittering death, as a child at some rare bauble."

—Edgar Allan Poe, *The Pit and the Pendulum*

Finding Moon's body must have been traumatic, yet Bridget Clogan stayed at Lahr House. She was still working there as late as 1915.[13] And while hotel employees see their share of uninspiring human behavior, for the Irish-born maid everything after room 41 was probably anticlimactic.

The space itself measured just twelve by fourteen feet (one writer calls it a "cubicle"), and upon entering from the hallway, the bed—its bedclothes undisturbed—was to the right, against the north wall. Opposite that, the south wall had a row of coat hooks screwed into it and the door opening into room 40. A window with louvered shutters was in the far wall across from the hall door, and the furnishing consisted of a plain Windsor chair, table, washstand, and no decorations apart from the spindle-work wooden bed frame and a picture hanging on the wall. The machine was arranged east to west, while Moon's body lay south to north, with his feet under the bed, the ax in his neck, and his head in a box.

Unlike the classic French guillotine, which uses a pulley,

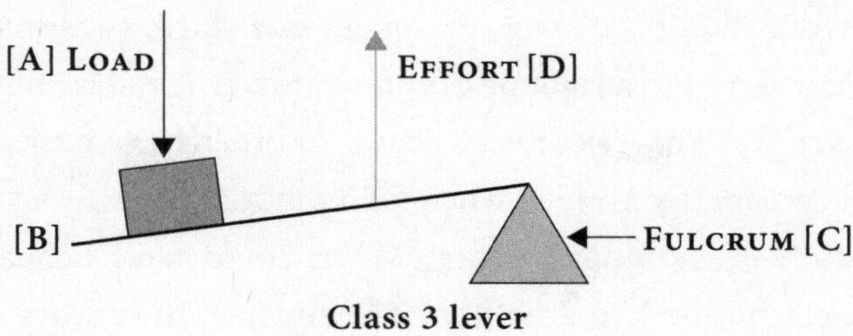

Class 3 lever

Moon's machine was a third-class lever—that is, a lever with one end resting on a fulcrum or pivot, and the other end supporting a load.

In Moon's device, the load [A] was the weighted ax head, and the lever [B], the seven-foot beam. The lever/beam is connected to the fulcrum [C], which was a wooden base screwed to the floor. Effort [D] is required to raise the load end six feet in the air and then, with the lever at a forty-five-degree angle from the wall and floor, it was secured in place with a double cord. Moon bolted a strong iron bracket with a hook on it into the window frame. The bracket was five feet above the floor, and one end of the double cord went through the hook in the bracket, and the other through an eyebolt screwed into the lever/beam.

When fully constructed, the lever was seven feet long and divided into three sections. The lower, wider two thirds were made of wood and attached to the base by means of a hinge to prevent any possible lateral motion. (One source states that the base was "two pieces of lumber, 1" x 6", and about six inches apart," though this sounds unnecessarily complicated.)[14]

The free end of the lever, the upper one third, consisted of the broadax and upright pieces of bar iron fastened with bolts and screws. They were very heavy, in order to give the machine great effectiveness when put in motion.[15]

With everything in place, Moon could have beheaded himself, but he had ambition. The nineteenth century saw surgery, childbirth, and dentistry become truly painless for the first time in human history, and the same could be done with autodecapitation. Furthermore, he had experience with anesthetics.

Three years earlier, Moon reportedly attempted suicide with chloroform in room 41, but hotel employees mistook the smell for coal gas and broke down the door. A doctor revived Moon, who was convulsing and later claimed that he took the drug to relieve cramps.[16] By 1876, he abandoned chloroform as a means of committing suicide and incorporated it into a larger plan in which he would drug himself into unconsciousness and use a delayed-release mechanism to free the ax.

The iron bracket Moon bolted to the window frame was fitted with a candleholder that allowed a candle to be inserted between the two strands of cord supporting the ax. It was positioned so the candle could burn for some time before reaching the cord, burning through it, and releasing the ax. (There are several different versions of how the candle and cord were arranged.) Moon put brown paper over the transom, presumably to keep stray drafts from interfering with the candle and perhaps to keep anyone from seeing what he was doing ("transom peeper" was once synonymous with "snoop").

In order to inhale the chloroform and keep his head and neck in place, Moon laid a wooden soapbox on its side and screwed it to the floor so that the box's opening was parallel with where the blade came to rest. The box's upper edge was shaved back so it would not interfere with the ax's progress, and cotton batting was put inside to absorb the chloroform.

To make sure that he did not change positions or otherwise disarrange the preparations while losing consciousness, Moon screwed a leather belt to the floor and used it to pinion his legs. The soapbox had two holes drilled opposite each other, and, after putting his head inside, he slipped a wooden dowel between them to hold his chin up. A block of pinewood was also screwed to the floor under the back of his neck, and this, along with the rod, kept his head in position before and after the beheading. Moon's final act might have been placing both hands under his suspender straps to keep them in place and, with that done, he stretched out, breathing in sweet heavy fumes, and waiting. (A picture taken by photographer P. W. Wolever shows the photographer's assistant posed like Moon, with the ax hovering overhead.)

Dr. Vinnedge believed Moon was no more than "somewhat stupefied" by the chloroform, while a Dr. Glick thought that it killed him; everything else, however, went according to plan; when the ax dropped, it severed the neck neatly and fully.[17] The resulting jets of blood pooled on the floor or were absorbed by his clothing and the batting.

Moon did not leave a note, but at some point he decided to lighten the proceedings with gallows humor, and wrote on the lever, *Kari kari, Patent applied for,* and *For sale or to let. Kari kari* was apparently his name for the device; it is believed that Moon was thinking of the word for Japanese ritual suicide, *hara kiri*. At the inquest, a witness testified that "Moon used that pet word or phrase penciled on the arm [of the machine]—'Karikari'—in conversation . . ."[18]

The Guillotine Show

Word of a suicide at Lahr House spread quickly, and crowds were already gathered at the hotel when Tippecanoe County coroner Dr. William W. Vinnedge arrived.

First, he examined the scene and the body, then impaneled a coroner's jury of prominent Lafayette citizens. They heard testimony about Moon's previous suicide attempts, including the 1873 incident, and another in which he first chloroformed and then tried asphyxiating himself in a hayrick. Hereditary insanity was possible since Moon's mother "was more than eccentric; she was remarkably peculiar" and his sister "was very much like his mother" and "would speak often and ably on strange subjects at the quiet Quaker meetings, and frequently appeared in gorgeous attire, so offensive to her sect."[19] Moon and his sister may have been unbalanced, but there also seems to be an element of rebellion in their behavior. Another witness recalled Moon's interest in inventing, particularly the possibility of perpetual motion, and a tendency for his mind to "'run on' methods of causing death, [and] . . . a great admiration for men who had rendered their names famous as inventors of machines which would cause death, suddenly and with dispatch."[20]

The jury decided that James Moon was mentally unstable and died by his own hands, but the circumstances were so unusual that the coroner spent two days studying the room and later wrote an article about it. (A formal autopsy might have explained another curious aspect of the case: Vinnedge estimated the time of death as seven A.M., yet ten hours in a small, hot, unventilated room had produced no visible signs of decay on the body.) He probably had to inform the widow as well, and Mary Moon did not take it well. Neighbors said her grief was beyond description and the thought of what Moon did "nearly destroys her reason."[21]

An undertaker named Caleb R. Scudder was authorized to remove the corpse, and he moved it across Main Street to his funeral parlor; Scudder also installed Moon's apparatus in an empty room in the Scudder Block. The body was claimed on Monday and buried that afternoon in the Farmers' Institute Cemetery under a sturdy, ogee-shaped headstone. Back at Lafayette, three thousand residents of the city and surrounding areas formed a "large, excitable, and noisy" crowd that turned out to see room 41, the places Moon visited on Saturday, and the bloodstained machine.[22] Morbid curiosity was doubtless part of the attraction, but Americans of the period were also fascinated by inventions.

Even as thousands descended on downtown Lafayette, *millions* were attending the Centennial International Exhibition at Philadelphia, a celebration of arts and sciences of the United States. Displays included the massive Corliss Centennial Steam Engine, Remington's typewriter, and Alexander Graham Bell's telephone, which, along with countless other useful devices, prompted the *London Times* to write that the "American invents as the Greek sculpted and the Italian painted. It is genius."[23]

This passion for technology may explain why newspapers printed such detailed descriptions of Moon's machine, as well as expressions of admiration. The admiration might be reluctant, like the author of a letter to the editor of the *Sunday Morning Leader* who pointed out how "[t]he idea was original and amazed the country . . . Such ingenuity, although fatal, should not sink into oblivion," or straightforward: "The sight and action of the machine amazed the most gigantic mind and heads of the Star City."[24] Interest in "Moon's Method" even extended overseas, with Britain's *Illustrated Police News* telling the story with a woodcut in their trademark penny-dreadful style.[25]

On Tuesday, Moon's oldest son, sixteen-year-old Arthur, arrived at Lafayette and angrily demanded the machine, which was disassembled, packed into the trunk, and hauled away to be destroyed. A man from Indianapolis reportedly tried to buy the device for $1,000, but the family refused all such offers, saying they would burn the lumber and bury the hardware (the determined entrepreneur then vowed to get a job on the neighboring farm so he could spy on the Moons and dig up the pieces). By Friday of that week it was back at Lafayette, apparently the property of Mr. Scudder, who was doing a good business charging the curious a nickel to see the Kari-kari. (Maybe the family came to a private arrangement with the undertaker, exchanging the machine for the coffin and funeral services.)

Mary Moon was criticized for allowing the exhibit ("Could anything be more revolting?"), but the widow had six children and a bisected husband to bury.[26] Sympathizers pointed out that the display "greatly helps a distressed and unsupported family, whom he left in deplorable circumstances!" (Moon might have even expected the machine to earn money and was half-joking when he wrote that it was "For sale or let.")[27]

The guillotine was shown in cities around Indiana, including Lebanon, Logansport, and Indianapolis, after which it was disassembled, placed in the original trunk, and stored in Caleb Scudder's attic. A reporter who inspected the pieces in 1880 saw dried blood on the blade and batting, which he described in an article that is the last known eyewitness description of the machine. It apparently went on tour for the last time in 1886 and its present whereabouts are unknown. (A novelist writing about Moon believes the machine might be in the Museum of Transport's collection at Kirkwood, Missouri.) Assuming the pieces were not swallowed up by fires, floods, or wartime scrap-metal drives so that Moon's creation ended up flying missions over Tokyo, it could well be in a dusty corner awaiting rediscovery, a unique artifact of death in nineteenth-century Indiana.

When the crowds thinned and the coroner left, the proprietor of Lahr House had room 41 locked, declaring that it would not be opened or rented for ten years. The building, however, underwent extensive renovations in the 1880s, and then again in 1998, when it was converted into the Historic Lahr Apartments.[28] There are stories about it being haunted, but these are mostly unrelated to the most notorious death on the premises.

A Bevy of Self-Beheaders

James Moon, of course, is not the only American to build a machine for cutting off his head.

In 1901, a man named Connelly decapitated himself in a cabin in California's Santa Cruz Mountains with either a broadax "in such a position that when he cut the cord the axe fell across his neck, stretched out on a block of wood," or "by allowing a huge saw with teeth filed off and edge ground to the sharpness of a razor, to fall upon his neck."[29] A Mr. Koetpnickger built a beheading machine in his apartment on Scholes Street in Brooklyn in 1894, but when it failed to work, he struck himself in the head with an ax and was hospitalized with a concussion.[30] A case similar to Moon's took place four years later in Chelsea, Massachusetts, in April 1880, when a thirty-year-old farmer named Stephen M. Pillsbury built a homemade guillotine in his father's barn.

He also used an ax blade, mounting it on a frame weighted with fifty pounds of stones; this frame moved up and down in the grooves of two tall wooden uprights. One upright was fitted with a lever on a pivot; a three-gallon tin watering pot was tied to one end of the lever, and its weight pushed up the other end of the lever, holding the frame, blade, and stones in place. A number of tiny holes were punched into the pot and, while the water dripped out, Pillsbury lay facedown between the uprights, inhaling ether. As the watering pot rose, the end supporting the frame dropped, until the blade was released and slid down the grooves and through Pillsbury's neck.

The citizens of Massachusetts were as interested in beheading as those of Indiana, and thousands went to see the guillotine. Newspapers were enthusiastic. "If anyone says the Yankees are not the most ingenious people in the world," wrote *The Illustrated Police News*, "and that the quality is not strong even in death, call his attention to Pillsbury's invention."[31] The machine did not go on display, though, and by July, Pillsbury's father was using "the axe that decapitated his son to cut wood and the uprights of the machine are used as side rails of a hot-bed at his farm, on which the deed was committed."[32]

Moon's death was somewhat different. He was presumably as unhappy as the long-unemployed Koetpnickynger, or Pillsbury, who apparently feared he was going mad, yet never seemed to express despair or hopelessness. There were also suicides in the family. Various sources claim that Moon's mother and sister killed themselves, that his brother shot himself at Indianapolis in 1881, that one of his sons attempted suicide with poison at Kansas City in 1900, and that his daughter Adella killed herself with gas in Chicago in 1911.[33] (In contrast, Moon's widow, the former Mary Fox, married a Mr. Dudleston in 1903, and lived another ten years. She is buried next to James.) While people commit suicide for different reasons, Moon is unusual for using it to achieve recognition.

On the face of it, self-beheading is an improbable route to celebrity. Looking at it from the perspective of Moon, who had "great admiration for men who had rendered their names famous as inventors of machines which could cause death" and believed that he could "make a better machine for taking life than has yet been invented," it makes a kind of sense.[34] And though he did not mention any inventors by name, he was probably referring to a thirty-eight-year-old French artisan named François Auguste Chere.

Chere moved from France to England after the Franco-

Prussian War and started a business that failed. He resolved to "quit the world" when he was penniless and in 1876, when Chere was living at London's New Cross Road, he bought some boards and a large, two-handled knife used by tanners for scraping hair off hides.[35] After he was not seen for a day, the door to his room was forced and Chere was found beheaded by a guillotine of his construction with stones tied to the blade for sufficient weight. The story was widely reported and for a brief time in February 1876, François Chere's name was known around the world.

There is no proof that Moon knew about Chere, but his own suicide took place just five months after the Frenchman's, and, of all the possible ways of bringing about death, Moon set out to improve decapitation. The result was a superior means of suicidal beheading, the Kari-kari.

Compact, easily stored, and transported, it could be quietly set up and torn down by one person using basic tools. Guillotines can be balky, but Moon's device has few moving parts to get out of order, and, assuming the candle and cord are properly arranged, autodecapitation can be done privately, painlessly, and with relatively little mess. Beyond such practical considerations, however, are elements that take both Chere's and Moon's machines into another realm and raises them from instruments to personal statements.

Guillotines and guillotine-like devices have a long history, but for the French the guillotine became more than a means of execution and represented the Enlightenment,

Revolution, and, like the fleur-de-lis or the Eiffel Tower, France itself. For Chere to kill himself with one in a foreign country was not just suicide but a proclamation of *"Je suis Francais!"* expressed in boards and blades. To an American the guillotine was not the "National Razor" or "Madam Guillotine" but a beheading machine and, like all machines, susceptible to improvement. If Chere's device is understood as a declaration of nationality, then Moon's might be one about sanity.

Mad Ambition?

The name *Moon* suggests *lunar* and *lunacy*, and a jury declared that James Moon was mad, pointing to his behavior and family history. Some suggested that wartime service in the 16th Indiana Battery Volunteers had unhinged Moon's mind, but the unit spent most of their time guarding Washington, D.C., and its eleven fatalities were from disease. Others thought Moon had "the face of a man of unsound mind"; phrenologists would doubtless have detected insanity in the shape of his skull, and modern writers in the difficult relationship with his father.[36]

Moon might have been mentally ill, yet he could not have committed suicide the way he did without clear thinking, long-range planning, and carefully orchestrating events to achieve a specific outcome. He seems to have realized that dying in an extraordinary manner was not enough, so he did it in downtown Lafayette, with its crowds and newspapers, inside a landmark hotel where Mark Twain and U. S. Grant had stayed and thereby associated his name with two of the most famous living Americans. There was also timing. Because he beheaded himself on the Sabbath, people were free to discuss what happened *and* he distracted them from church.

Did James Moon get what he wanted? The man who never did anything worth mentioning apart from killing himself was discussed on both sides of the Atlantic, his invention went on tour, and he is remembered when arguably worthier contemporaries are not. In short, his suicide must be accounted a perverse and somewhat tawdry success. Only Moon knows if it was worth it.

The Man in Room 13

Today, Moon is an oddity in the history of Tippecanoe County history, but he became a legend in the lodging trade.

In 1889, humorist Edgar W. "Bill" Nye heard a story from a bellboy, who heard it from another bellboy, who claimed to have once worked at Lahr House. Nye's informant said a man had rented room 13 at the hotel and that he was "a kind of inventor, somehow":

He had been staying at the Lahr House a week or so, I believe, and carrying up tools and pieces of board and stuff because he was building some kind of a machine and was quiet about it for fear someone would beat him on the patent, he said.

The man did not respond to being called and the bellboy was finally put over the transom. He unlocked the door from the inside and came out looking "quite pale."

No. 13 had, it seems, got his machine done the night before, and had tried it to see if it would work. It was a kind of meat axe running in a groove like the French do—funny, and it was hung with a cord and trigger, fixed so that a little thread that run the trigger was pulled through a wax candle. A man could load up with morphine, or something kind of soothing like that, lay down with his head on the upholstered headrest, light the candle and go to sleep. He had greased up the running glass of the thing and then begun to experiment. It worked first rate. They didn't have any autopsy. Friends thought it wasn't really necessary.[37]

James Moon had become part of hotel lore: the archetypal "Guest Found Horribly Dead."

Bigfoot's Gold: The Secret of Ape Canyon

One night in the summer of 1924, a small group of angry, rock-throwing, ape-men attacked a cabin with five miners inside, near Mt. St. Helens, Washington. While most Sasquatch are content to stare at human beings and then vanish into the woods, these creatures seemed determined to get in and commit mayhem. It was unusual behavior for Bigfoot and the culmination of a series of strange events involving séances, spirits, and gold mining. Depending on one's perspective, what happened at Ape Canyon is either baffling and unique or utterly predictable, a twentieth-century example of a very old kind of story, not usually associated with our most prominent cryptid.

Thousands of encounters with hairy giants or their footprints have been recorded in North America, a handful of which have become famous. These include the Patterson-Gimlin film, Jerry Crew's plaster casts, William Roe's detailed sighting, Albert Ostman's abduction, Ape Canyon, and a few other, more or less arguable, classics.

For scientifically minded Bigfoot investigators, these incidents involve living, breathing beings, possibly primitive men or apelike bipeds, which are no more paranormal than mule deer or yellow-bellied marmots. To Fred Beck, one of the miners at Ape Canyon the creatures were something very different.

It was not because their behavior was unusual. Bigfoot seldom threaten human beings, yet chimpanzees carry out organized hunts for red colobus monkeys, so there is no obvious reason why ape-men could not launch a coordinated assault on five of their small pink cousins.[1] What makes Ape Canyon unpalatable for those who want Bigfoot hunting to be scientific is the firsthand account published by Beck in 1967, titled *I Fought the Apemen of Mt. St. Helens*.

The booklet opens with a description of how the cabin was besieged by ape-men, and goes on to explain that the creatures were actually "manifestations," and just one of the many psychic phenomena experienced by the miners. Furthermore, they were Spiritualists who searched for gold with the help of spirits and saw visions. Beck describes childhood encounters with mysterious beings, discusses metaphysics, and makes passing references to flying saucers, the Fall of Man, and Ascended Masters. Taken together, they make *I*

Fought the Apemen the redheaded stepchild of Sasquatch literature.

Anything involving Bigfoot attracts the attention of cryptozoologists and the story has always been discussed in the context of cryptozoology, the study of "hidden animals." This is a scientific approach to creatures that might exist, like Bigfoot or the Loch Ness Monster, familiar species that appear outside their normal ranges (e.g., kangaroos in Wisconsin), and animals like the thylacine, which have been declared extinct, but could still survive. This chapter is an attempt to take *I Fought the Apemen* out of cryptozoology and consider Fred Beck's account as a tale belonging to another, older tradition.

The Becks

Beck's account is curious mixture of frontier life and mysticism, and reflects his background.

In 1880, William T. Beck; his wife, Ella; and their three small sons, Albert, John, and Jesse, arrived in the Washington Territory from Kansas.[2] They moved several times but mainly lived at Kelso, in Cowlitz County, a lumber town with so many taverns and brothels that it was called "Little Chicago." (In 1956, the chamber of commerce came up with the more wholesome sobriquet "Kelso, Smelt Capital of the World," but the smelts ran out and it is now known as the

"City of Friendly People.")[3] Mr. Beck planted apple trees and worked as a logger, so he was often away while his wife taught Sunday school, gave music lessons, and was active in Grand Army of the Republic veterans' affairs. The Beck family also grew; Georgianna was born in 1880, William in 1885, Alfred and his twin brother, Edwin, on July 22, 1888 (Edwin died in infancy), and Arthur in 1891. Arthur wrote a series of reminiscences about his family's history and life at Cowlitz County when it was still the frontier.

He described his mother as a "real pioneer woman" who helped deliver babies and "[t]o give the reader an insight as to how rugged life was in the early years . . . Coming home from school one day about 1898, I found my brother John seated on the porch sewing up a three-inch ax cut in his knee, using a darning needle and white cotton thread. If you doubt that requires grit, try it on your own knee."[4] School was four months a year, and a photograph taken in 1900 shows Miss Hargraves and her class from the Lower Coweeman School, with the younger boys wearing Little Lord Fauntleroy suits, the girls in pinafores, and all twenty-three students looking horribly serious except for Fred and Arthur Beck, who are smiling.[5] According to *I Fought the Apemen*, Fred was already having visions, and it is not surprising that the twelve-year-old clairvoyant stands somewhat apart from the group.

Even ordinary childhood incidents could be mysterious for the young Beck:

> When just a boy I was in the pasture playing with my beanshooter. I had bought it with some long earned coins. It had a twisted wire handle. I lost it, and as I was crying, a kindly woman came up to me and put her arms around me. I felt warm all over. "Little boy," she said, "don't cry. Go home, you will find your beanshooter there."
>
> I went home and found it, and as far as I knew then it was the same one. But years later I found the one I lost. It was weather beaten and the rubber was rotten.

Another woman was invisible to everyone except Fred:

> I would be sleeping on the hard benches of the Adventist Church my folks used to attend, and I would have my head in a lady's lap, only when I mentioned it to my folks, they said there was no one else there and took it to be a boy's musings.

As the Becks matured they worked in blacksmith shops and mills and at various lumber camps. Logging was "more dangerous than war," and William, the fourth-born son, was killed in an accident in 1909.[6] At age twenty-two, Fred operated a donkey engine—a mechanical winch used for dragging heavy logs—and had his first encounter with an ape-man while working at a lumber camp near Kelso.

> One night I heard a rustling outside, and I heard something pushing its way under our tent. A tall hairy figure stood before us watching us. It scared my brother, who afterward said it was a large bear. But I have seen enough bears to know that it was no bear. There was nothing else he knew to call it.[7]

It was around this time that Beck "became immersed in spiritualism," the popular belief that the personality survives death and that it was possible to communicate with those who have passed on.

How he became involved is unknown, but it was typical, for "[t]hroughout his life, he espoused novel beliefs."[8] Meetings were held, and in time Beck "created a following of folks who sometimes gathered for séances. Some of his own brothers and his sister were intrigued with this activity. They enjoyed the experiences but their spouses were chagrined."[9]

Like Adventism and the Latter-day Saints movement, Spiritualism emerged from the religious revivals and social reform movements that "blazed" across upper and western New York State until the area was known as the "Burned-Over District." It began at rural Hydesville in 1848 with the Fox sisters, two girls who figured out how to communicate with a spirit haunting their farmhouse; from there it spread around the world with astonishing speed. Conversing with ghosts was not unprecedented: Twenty-seven years before Hydesville, a poltergeist spoke audibly, and insultingly, to the people of Adams, Tennessee, answering their questions and making predictions. It haunted the Bell family and, since witchcraft was believed to be responsible for poltergeists, was known as the "Bell Witch." Spiritualists accepted the reality of such phenomena but not the traditional explanations.

Since Spiritualism "investigates, analyzes, and classifies facts and manifestations demonstrated from the Spirit side of Life," it was scientific, a constituted sort of Industrial Revolution of the spirit comparable to the other developments transforming nineteenth-century life.[10] For believers, 1848 marked the beginning of a new era in which the veil that separated the living and dead was lifted and one could converse "with angels and spirits as man with man."[11] The possibilities seemed limitless, and Article 2 of the 1876 *Platform and Constitution of the New Hampshire State Convention of Spiritualists* stresses the application of Spiritualism to "practical life," which would certainly include finding your own gold mine.[12]

Seance in the Pines

The prospectors were Fred Beck; his father-in-law, Marion Lefever Smith (called "Hank" in *I Fought the Apemen*); Smith's nineteen-year-old son, LeRoy; Gabe Lefever (probably Smith's cousin or nephew); John Peterson; and an unnamed man not present when the apes attacked.

Beck does not describe how they actually looked for gold beyond calling it "psychic," though a contemporary newspaper states, "It is said all five men are Spiritualists and hold frequent séances in the woods."[13] Each member of the party was "psychically sensitive," but as someone with experience in Spiritualist meetings, it is reasonable to assume that Beck played a leading role as medium.

Mediumship is the psychic ability to communicate with discarnate intelligences, including gods, angels, and spirits of the dead, through various mental and physical means. Mental mediums use automatic writing, automatic speech, clairaudience (psychically "hearing" voices, music, etc.), and inner visions, while physical mediums produce the more spectacular external phenomena: object movement, audible sounds and voices, levitation, ectoplasm (a polymorphic substance from the medium's body), production of apports (solid objects like fruit, flowers, or live animals), and the materialization of spirits. Beck and his party experienced a variety of physical manifestations during their years at Mt. St. Helens.

One Comforting and One Great Spirit

The men began prospecting in 1916 reportedly by holding séances and contacting spirits. They included "Vander White," who was a "comforting friend" but not much help in finding gold mines, and a second being that did not manifest until August 1922, but showed them where to dig. According to *I Fought the Apemen*, a large Indian dressed in buckskin appeared to us and talked to us. He was the picture of stateliness itself. He never told us his name, but we always called him the Great Spirit. He replied once, "The Great Spirit is above me. We are all of the Great Spirit, if we listen when the Great Spirit talks."

More to the point:

> The big Indian being told us there would be a white arrow [going] before us. Another man, who was not present during the attack in 1924, could see the arrow easily and clearly at all times. And I could see it nearly as well.
>
> So we started by the Lewis River, south of Mt. St. Helens, and went up the Muddy River, and in all we followed the white arrow four days. The going was slow, for in those days it was very rugged territory. Hank's temper was growing short as he climbed the hills. He had always been a believer of spiritual things, and afterwards he was a believer. But he lost his temper and cussed. He swore at the spirit leading us. His face was red and we could not stop him: "Just a wild goose chase," he exclaimed, "they lied to us, and got us running all over the hills, and I want nothing more to do with them." He went on and on.

If any member of the group could be called their leader, it is "Hank," Marion Smith. He was older (b. 1866), and the father, father-in-law, and possibly uncle, to three of the men, as well as a "great hunter and good woodsman." His impatience and lack of self-control, however, was their undoing.

> Then just when he [Smith] had started to calm down, we all saw the arrow soar up high, change direction and swoop down. We had to follow in the general direction before we could find it again. It hovered near the top of the north cliff of Ape Canyon. That was the site where we later blasted out our shaft.
>
> We got a little closer, and we all saw the image of a large door open, and the big Indian appeared in front of it. He spoke: "Because you have cursed the spirit leading you, you will be shown where there is gold, but it is not given to you."
>
> With those words, he disappeared. Then we saw the door slowly close. There was a huge lock and latch, but as the door shut, the lock did not latch: a closed door but it was not locked! "We just as well pack up and go home," one of the party said.

After six years of looking, though, the temptation to dig proved irresistible, and they decided to make a claim. It required a written description and they had nothing to write with, not until a pencil spontaneously materialized, or apported, into Fred's hand. Mabel Beck later recognized the pencil as one she bought when her husband was away. (Their four-year-old son Francis had been chewing on it, so she put the pencil away in a drawer, from which it later vanished.) On September 2, 1922, Beck and Smith filed a location notice for a mine named the Vander White, in honor of their spirit friend.[14]

It was located on a cliff side and the men had to lower themselves on ropes to reach a narrow ledge, which was enlarged with dynamite. From there they began burrowing into the canyon's north wall. Despite this apparent progress they felt as though the venture would fail, a disquiet that reflects one of the failures of Spiritualism.

In separating themselves from superstition with its primitive, often grotesque, elements, the Spiritualists also abandoned its wealth of accumulated knowledge. One result of this was seen at Mt. St. Helens, where the mediums-cum-miners repeatedly made mistakes that were addressed, if not always solved, by countless generations of traditional magical treasure hunters. By the first quarter of the twentieth century, old-fashioned "money-diggers" were thin on the ground, but America once had them in abundance.

Treasure hunting was part of the European magical tradition and remained a popular, if little discussed, pursuit in the United States until the twentieth century. Small groups went out at night to perform ceremonies that revealed the whereabouts of treasure, casting spells that protected them from the supernatural forces standing guard.

Though treasure hunting was seldom successful, its practitioners would have understood exactly what was happening at Mt. St. Helens.

More Oddities

Beyond the daily round of séances, phantom arrows, and apports, Fred Beck found time to have unusual experiences on his own.

At some point he was off by himself and feeling lonely when a young woman appeared. They chatted and Beck was invited to visit the campsite she shared with her father.

> When I arrived at her camp, I did not see her father, and never did see him. She had a fire going, and a light colored blanket was spread out and she was sitting on it. It was a warm summer evening, and we held another pleasant conversation. I remember her telling me how she liked the fresh air of the mountains, and how wonderfully she loved nature.
>
> She would be talking on a subject, then pause and say, "Isn't that right, Dad?" This she said several times. There was no tent, cooking utensils, no food, and certaiply [*sic*]

> no visible father. The most amazing thing was I did not at the time think her different than any other person. When she spoke to her invisible Dad, I felt just like her Dad was there.
>
> I left her and walked back to camp, but my mind seemed like it was a thousand miles away. I could hear the other men talking, but it seemed like they were below me, and their voices sounded soft and distant.
>
> I do not know anyone who had seen her but myself.

Beck was the only miner to enjoy a pleasantly surreal night out, but the group experienced other phenomena together. Thumping sounds were heard inside the earth and footprints discovered whose size and origin defied explanation.

> There in the center of the sand bar were two huge tracks [nineteen inches long and] about four inches deep. There was not another track on that sand bar!
>
> There we were standing in the middle of the sand bar, and not one of us could conceive any earthly thing taking steps 160 feet long. "No human being could have made these tracks," Hank said, "and there's only one way they could be made, something dropped from the sky and went back up."

Though the prints made Marion Smith uneasy, "no one was really worried about the tracks as regarding any threat to our safety." Nor was it fear of the footprints' makers that led to the men building a permanent dwelling; they had been living in a tent, but mining required more supplies and equipment and a safe place to store them.

With endless amounts of raw material available, the men turned pine trees into squared-off logs, piled them into thick windowless walls, and chinked the spaces between with pine branches. The roof was built to withstand heavy snow, a stone fireplace provided heat, and water came from a spring a hundred yards away. They did not know it at the time, but the cabin was strong enough to withstand both the elements, and the residents, of Mt. St. Helens.

Gold and Gorillas

In July 1924, ore samples from the Vander White were assayed, and the claim's value estimated at approximately $2,000 a ton; if this proved accurate, the miners were on the verge of becoming rich men. Any anticipatory pleasure Beck felt was dulled by a toothache, and when he asked his father-in-law to drive him into town to get it pulled, the older man replied that "'God or the Devil' could not get him [Smith] away from there." It was also around this time that the thumping noises grew louder and more insistent.

For about a week they heard booming, "like something was hitting its self on its chest," which was joined by a "shrill peculiar whistle each evening . . . coming from one ridge, and then . . . an answering whistling from another ridge."[15]

The sounds made Smith wary. He carried his Remington automatic when going for water on July 11 and asked Fred to accompany him and bring his .30-.30 Winchester.[16] According to the July 18, 1924, *Kelsonian*, they were on their way to the spring when a figure appeared on the other side of a small canyon, a hairy blackish-brown creature standing seven feet tall. Smith yelled and raised his rifle, and it dodged behind a pine tree. When the beast peeked around the trunk, he fired three times and exclaimed, "Don't worry about that devil, Fred, I got him right in the head!" The devil had a hard head and it reappeared two hundred yards away, running "fast and upright," giving Fred the chance to loose three more shots before the retreating figure was out of sight.

The men returned with water and told the others what happened, and everyone agreed that it was time to go. Smith's Ford was too far away for them to reach it before sundown, and not liking the idea of being in the woods after dark, they decided to wait till morning. After dinner they smoked their pipes, fastened the door shut, and went to bed: two in a bunk built into the wall and the rest on pine boughs on the floor.

Between cooking, smoking, and unwashed clothes, the atmosphere in the cabin must have been close, yet its inmates doubtless slept better having thick walls between themselves and the moonlit forest.

Night of the Mountain Devils

The assault began around midnight and, according to *I Fought the Apemen*, it started with a bang. Something struck the cabin with enough force to dislodge the chinking from between two of the logs onto Marion Smith and jolt the men awake. Smith was yelling, kicking, and waving his rifle, and, as Fred cleaned the debris off him, they heard what sounded like "a great number of feet trampling and rattling over a pile of our unused shakes." Everyone grabbed a pistol or rifle, and Beck and Smith looked through the space where the chinking had been and saw ape-men outside. The cabin was being pelted with rocks, and the miners improvised a plan to defend themselves.

> The only time we shot our guns that night was when the creatures were attacking our cabin. When they would quiet down for a few minutes, we would quit shooting. I told the rest of the party, that maybe if they saw we were only shooting when they attacked, they might realize we were only defending ourselves. We could have had clear shots at them through the opening left by the chinking had we chosen to shoot. We did shoot, however, when they climbed up on our roof. We shot round after round through the roof. We had to brace the hewed-logged door with a long pole taken from the bunk bed. The creatures

were pushing against it and the whole door vibrated from the impact. We responded by firing many more rounds through the door. They pushed against the walls of the cabin as if trying to push the cabin over, but this was pretty much an impossibility, as previously stated the cabin was a sturdy made building. Hank and I did most of the shooting—the rest of the party crowded to the far end of the cabin, guns in their hands. One had a pistol, which still is in my family's possession, the others clutched their rifles. They seemed stunned and incredulous.

A humorous thing I well remember was Hank singing: "If you leave us alone, we'll leave you alone, and we'll all go home in the morning." He did not mean it to be humorous, for Hank was dead serious, and sang under the impression that the "Mountain Devils" as he called them, might understand and go away.

At one point a hairy hand reached through the opening in the wall and grabbed an ax by the handle; Fred "swiftly turned the head of the axe upright, so that it caught on the logs; and at the same time Hank shot, barely missing my hand . . . [the] creature let go, and I pulled the handle back in, and put the axe in a safe place.[17]

They never saw more than three creatures at once, and there were quiet intervals, but the attacks continued until just before dawn, at which point the apes withdrew. When it was light enough to see clearly, the men ventured out and saw one of the creatures standing at the edge of the canyon eighty yards away. Whether it was a straggler from the night before or an innocent giant hairy bystander, the men were not taking chances and Beck fired three times, toppling it over the cliff and down a gorge four hundred feet deep.[18]

Taking nothing but their packs and firearms, the men abandoned the cabin along with "about two hundred dollars in supplies, powder, and drilling equipment."

As they drove down the mountain, Fred suggested that they keep the attack a secret. Everyone agreed, including Marion Smith, who immediately told the rangers at Spirit Lake and then his friends in the Blue Ox Tavern at Kelso. According to Fred's son, Clifford, "my grandfather went down to the corner tavern and got a snootful. He blabbed the whole story."[19]

Sportsmen, reporters, and police converged on Mt. St. Helens in what became known as the Great Ape Hunt of 1924. The woods were full of people "armed with rifles and shotguns and pistols, and they're shooting at anything that moves."[20] Beck returned with two reporters and a detective to find the miners' possessions strewn about the cabin, the blasting powder missing, and at least one giant footprint. It was photographed, and pictures were taken of Fred and LeRoy Smith reenacting the siege.

Many dismissed the story as a hoax. Deputy game warden Justus Murk declared it was "[a]ll bunk."[21] When forest rangers J. H. Huffman and W. M. Welch found a four-toed footprint, "Huffman . . . with the knuckles and palm of his right hand duplicated the imprint perfectly with the statement: 'They were made that way.'"[22] Over the years, the attack would be dismissed as either a hoax or a figment of the miners' imagination. It could have been group hysteria brought on by a rockslide, teenagers from the nearby YMCA summer camp rolling stones into the canyon, or prankster Rant Mullens, who claimed that he and his friends threw rocks at the cabin and made the tracks with giant carved wooden feet.

Wildly exaggerated versions of the story also appeared in print. On July 14, 1924, the *Berkeley (CA) Daily Gazette* reported that the miners were surrounded by "a cordon of thirty gorillas" and "200 rocks crashed through the roof to the floor of the shack." Newspapers also printed allegedly authentic Indian legends about mountain giants and renegade tribes, "much like giant apes in appearance who lived like wild animals in the secluded caves of the High Cascades."[23]

While reporters turned in their copy, Fred got his tooth pulled. He was leaving the dentist when a group of Yakima Indians told Beck about the "Selahtiks," beings that were "not like a man and not like a spirit, but in between."[24]

They traveled the mountain ranges, floated down rivers at night "like logs," and ran off with Indian women. Fred learned that if he ever saw one "to make sure I expressed to them that I was friendly [by taking] some cedar boughs and [waving] it at them, and in that way they would know I had come in peace." The Yakima also told Beck something he already knew—ape-men hold grudges: "'If you ever harm one they will get even . . . They never forget.'"[25]

Nor was the miners' adventure likely to be forgotten around Mt. St. Helens, where it is preserved in local folklore and geography. The narrow gorge where the attack occurred has been "Ape Canyon" since 1924, and when an immense lava tube was discovered nearby in 1951, it was christened "Ape Cave."[26] Meanwhile, Fred Beck returned to a more or less ordinary routine of work, family, and psychic experiments.

After the Apes

Traumatic Sasquatch encounters have been known to sour people on the outdoors. When a Nootka trapper named Muchalat Harry was kidnapped by hairy giants in 1928, he escaped but never left his village again. There is nothing to suggest that Fred Beck suffered similar long-term effects, and though little has been written about his life after Ape Canyon, members of the Beck family tend to put their thoughts on paper.

> Our Uncle Fred impressed us. There was [a] uniqueness about him that filled the three of us with awe. It was our feeling that he could read our innermost thoughts.

> As a child, I always tried to keep a chair between Uncle Fred and me. I felt he had "x-ray eyes," remembers June. "I didn't want him looking through me!"
>
> The fifth son of the William Becks did seem to have currents of energy that were lacking in the other Becks. He seemed engrossed in various phases of "psychic phenomena."[27]

There is no evidence that Beck continued to hold séances or prospect for gold, but he did pursue an interest in psychic healing. Ronald Beck told a friend that "his Father [*sic*] Fred was very similar to Edgar Casy [Cayce]. He claimed Fred had psychic powers. That he could go into a trance and predict things."[28] (Edgar Cayce [1877–1945], "the Sleeping Prophet," gave countless trance readings. Most concerned people's health, with occasional departures into more arcane subjects, like Atlantis.) Some of Fred's family found the "faith-healing period" embarrassing.

> Strangers drove out the Coweeman valley road looking for the residence of Dr. Beck. They came from places out of state and stopped to ask for direction to the "Doctor."
>
> Well, our Uncle Fred was a self-appointed doctor. We didn't think of him as a real doctor so we tended to look the other way and ignore the requests. However, our parents politely gave out directions to the Alfred Beck home.[29]

At some point, Beck also overcame his reluctance to discuss what happened at Mt. St. Helens and "delighted in telling the story to family members whenever he got the chance."[30] One history includes this unexpected detail:

> Clifford said his dad received a telegram from the Federal Bureau of Investigation Washington, D.C. He remembers reading it. "Do not shoot the creatures [ape-men]. The Federal Government knows all about them. They are on official record." Or words to that effect, Cliff added.[31]

For those around him, living "in the same neighborhood as Uncle Fred added excitement to a quiet community," but Beck was not just a mystic. In 1956 he still worked at a Weyerhauser mill (producers of wood and paper) and continued there until around 1960, when his wife died and he was seventy-two years old.[32]

The Birth of Bigfoot Hunting

The attack at Ape Canyon remains a unique event, but the "Hairy Ape Hunt" that followed was not. Three years before Mt. St. Helens, Pennsylvanians were pursuing the "Gettysburg Gorilla," and in 1931 there was a search for a short hairy creature on Long Island, New York. Ralston, Mississippi, had a "gorilla hunt" in 1952; a posse chased a peach-eating "Booger" at Clanton, Alabama, in 1960; and carloads of armed hunters set out after Texas's "Lake Worth Monster" in 1969. Similar ad hoc expeditions have taken place around the country, but it was the development of a more systematic approach to finding ape-men that led colorful old Uncle Fred to turn his colorful old story into a book.

In British Columbia during the mid-1950s, the Swiss emigrant Rene Dahinden and journalist John Green began a long-term, open-ended search for Sasquatch. Working independently and together, they interviewed witnesses and studied footprints and physical evidence, slowly piecing together a profile of the creatures as a species of bipedal primate. Hairy giants went from a regional to a national story in 1958, when enormous tracks appeared at a road construction site outside Bluff Creek, California.

A bulldozer operator named Jerry Crew poured plaster into the prints, and the *Humboldt Times* ran a photograph of him holding the cast of what looks like the bottom of a flat, human-looking foot, sixteen inches long with potato-sized toes. The Associated Press picked up the story, and the whole country was soon aware of "Big Foot."

Scottish-born naturalist Ivan Sanderson followed with a magazine piece, "The Strange Story of America's Abominable Snowman" (*True Magazine*, December 1959), which contains a detailed account of Crew's story and suggests that something like the Himalayan yeti lives in the Pacific North-west. Sanderson wrote other articles about incidents from British Columbia, including William Roe's sighting of a female Sasquatch at Mica Mountain in 1955, and the Chapman family's encounter with a Bigfoot at Ruby Creek in 1941. As the public read about these events, most for the first time, investigators reexamined old cases like Ape Canyon and visited Fred Beck, the one witness willing to discuss it.

The Irish big-game hunter Peter Byrne claims to have spoken with him as early as 1960, but Byrne's account contains unlikely errors such as Beck claiming not to know what happened to the other men who were present in 1924. (Byrne also reports that the remains of the miners' cabin were still standing in 1972.)

Six years later Beck was interviewed by Roger Patterson, a rodeo cowboy from Yakima, Washington. Patterson's search for Bigfoot began after reading Sanderson's articles, and he quizzed the old man several times about Ape Canyon, the creatures, and their footprints. He wrote it up, added some embellishments ("Tremendous boulders began pelting their cabin roof followed by loud wailing that echoed hideously off the canyon walls"), and told the story in his 1966 book *Do Abominable Snowmen of America Really Exist?* Rene Dahinden met Beck around 1968, and John Green sometime in the late 1960s.

Green's interview did not go well. Though he believes that "something exciting" happened to the miners, "Fred Beck had told his story so often that he had established a set pattern of things and there wasn't much use in asking further questions."[33] This agrees with Beck's nieces' account. They describe how at one "point Uncle Fred always closed his eyes as if to get a better look," and at another, "Uncle Fred always sighed here and brushed his right hand over his head."[34]

Decades later, John Green remembers the meeting with Beck as something out of the ordinary:

> I can recall talking to Fred Beck only once and it was a long time ago, my recollections are fragmentary, but I think I would remember if he had said anything about spiritualism, the occult etc. and I do not. What I do recall is that his son took a major role in the latter part of our conversation and insisted on showing me a photograph that he said included the image of someone who was not actually there . . .[35]

When Beck was a very old man he appeared in a documentary describing the creatures as having "big, big shoulders and small hips, and hairy . . . they looked like they was eight, nine, feet tall."[36] The ape-men might have grown over time, but physical details were less important to Fred Beck than what Ape Canyon revealed about the creatures' *true* nature. None of the Bigfoot hunters seemed interested in that aspect of the story, however, so Beck felt "it right that I express my views at last" and tell "the real facts after 43 years of silence" in a book.[37]

He dictated the story to his son Ronald, who later wrote, "I was close to my father, and believe me, his account is straight and true," but also told a friend that "the book was his [Ronald's] interpretation on his Father's story."[38] Do the contents of *I Fought the Apemen* reflect the elder Beck's beliefs?

Michael Perry, Fred's nephew, has "no doubts about Fred and his son Ronald discussing the [metaphysical] theory, but those words were written by Ron—Fred never talked like that."[39] John Green had the same response: "When I later read the *I Fought* . . . book my reaction was that it was more the son's book than Fred's. I presume that son was Ronald . . ."[40] By all accounts, Ronald held his father in high regard, and it is reasonable to assume that the results are a fair presentation of the elder Beck's ideas, if not his idiom. Since it is impossible to know who believed what, Fred will be referred to as the sole author. (Ronald died in September 2009, a month before work on this chapter began. Since it is impossible to know who believed what, Fred will be referred to as the sole author.)

The Metaphysics of Ape-Men

I Fought the Apemen is a patchwork: part memoir, part history, and part metaphysical disquisition. Its twenty-two pages are divided into five sections: "The Attack" is Beck's account of the siege, followed by a newspaper article, "Legendary

Mt. St. Helens Apemen Called Legitimate"[41]; "Background Events" describes Fred's early mystical experiences; "Questions and Answers" offers amusing anecdotes about the miners' time in the mountains, such as shooting rats off a sack of dynamite, and useful advice like "If you boil beans in the mountains, put on a good lid and be patient." Beck describes the ape-men as physical and spiritual beings and believes that UFOs expand consciousness by "confounding the wisdom of the proud and material minded" (he was probably familiar with the Maury Island incident, which involved doughnut-shaped UFOs that appeared sixty miles northeast of Kelso in June 1947). "Miscellaneous Selections" elaborates on events at Ape Canyon, and the booklet closes with "Theories on the Origin of Abominable Snowmen," which describes Earth in prehistoric times, Native American folklore, other Bigfoot encounters, and reflections on esoteric beliefs and higher consciousness.

For this discussion, the crucial point about Fred's metaphysical beliefs is that ape-men are a paranormal phenomenon, a concept that would not raise an eyebrow among the Yakima but was something new for white men. What he believed requires some explanation, and even then Fred found it "hard to classify a spiritual subject and apply a system to it."

Like many mystics, Beck sees the cosmos as consisting of many spheres, dimensions, or planes of existence. The different planes are often depicted as layers, with the physical, or material, plane—the universe inhabited by humankind—sandwiched between higher and lower *immaterial* planes. All of them are inhabited by beings whose level of spiritual development, or consciousness, is consistent with the plane upon which they exist; beings with a primitive consciousness exist on lower levels, and those with higher consciousness in higher ones. Though the planes are separate, they overlap, and under certain circumstances nonphysical beings from other planes can manifest in the physical world.

One reason they might do this is an impulse common to all life, on every plane: the urge to evolve. This is not evolution in the sense of adapting to the environment but movement toward a higher form of consciousness, and ultimately, to the highest form of consciousness, which is human.

"Humanity," however, is more than the Homo sapiens who exist in the material plane, for the inhabitants of higher, nonphysical planes like Vander White and the Great Spirit, are also human. Moreover, the level of a spirit's consciousness determines how it will manifest in the physical world. Highly evolved spirits take noble and beautiful human forms, while beings with primitive consciousnesses from lower planes appear in crude or monstrous shapes.

Beck thought it was the miners' activities that first attracted the Sasquatch's attention, particularly blasting with dynamite. Since the ape-men's plane of existence is close to the material world, and the division between planes is thinner in the mountains, the creatures might have been watching the men invisibly. Curiosity and the impulse to evolve would have drawn them toward the miners' human consciousnesses and the earthly plane they inhabit.

The ape-men's manifestation seems to have been gradual, beginning with sounds and intermittent materializations that could have produced the solitary footprints in the sandbar. Perhaps the process was similar to what Col. Norbert Okolowicz and Dr. Gustave Geley witnessed at a series of séances by the Polish medium Teofil Modrzejewski.

Between 1919 and 1925, Modrzejewski, better known as "Franek Kluski" ("Frank Noodles," a name he might have adopted because mediums were not quite respectable) produced a number of remarkable materializations during his sittings, including animals that felt solid, gave off strong smells, and interacted with the sitters and surroundings. They included a hawk, an animal like a miniature lion, and an ape-man that the participants named "Primordial Man" or "Pithecanthropus."

Pithecanthropus first appeared in 1919 as a bundle of tangled hair accompanied by "smacking" sounds, it intrigued the sitters, which likely hastened its development. While the creatures at Mt. St. Helens stood about seven feet tall, had stout frames "more like a giant human than an ape," and were "hairy but not shaggy," Kluski's ape-man was something different. A photograph shows a smallish figure obscured by what looks like black gauze, but the fully realized Pithecanthropus had long, coarse, curly brown hair with patches of gray and was strong enough to carry a fully loaded bookcase around the room. Its occasional outbursts of wild behavior could be frightening, but no one was ever threatened or harmed and the ape-man was so good-natured that it had to be discouraged from licking the sitters. Over time Pithecanthropus lost cohesion, reverted to smacking sounds, and finally vanished.

Though ape-men can be physically imposing and enormously strong, Beck considered them transients on the material plane, temporary constructs created by a "vibration of power and certain fine substances," whose bodies do not survive the spirit's return to its own dimension. The "fine substances" of which they are composed presumably disperse, and tangible proof of their existence disappears.

The mechanics of ape-man materialization are obscure, yet their motives at Ape Canyon appear straightforward; what began with natural attraction to the miners' consciousnesses was followed by retaliation at the miners' unprovoked violence. "Our mistake," Beck writes, "was shooting them."

I Fought the Apemen of Mt. St. Helens was privately printed in 1967, but few people saw it, or a later edition, and Fred Beck's mystical explorations remain "a bit of a 'taboo' subject with conventional researchers."[42] The only firsthand written account of Ape Canyon could not be ignored, though, and a sort of compromise emerged.

Rene Dahinden is a good example of a researcher who was notably impatient with the paranormal. A story is told about him following giant footprints that abruptly ended in the middle of a field. Someone suggested, jokingly perhaps, that the Bigfoot flew away, and Dahinden turned and left without saying a word. Nevertheless, the notoriously prickly Canadian interviewed Beck, wrote about Ape Canyon, read all of *I Fought the Apemen*, and even brought out a new edition. Like many others he probably "concluded that Fred had gone a little strange in his old age" and "*just ignored the paranormal stuff.*"[43]

Fred Beck died on June 1, 1972, at age eighty-three, and since then a new generation of enthusiasts has appeared for whom the history of Bigfoot began at Bluff Creek, California, in 1967, when Roger Patterson and Bob Gimlin filmed a female Sasquatch. With new cases to investigate and technologies to apply, Ape Canyon is a low priority, and, as Loren Coleman points out: "[W]hat exactly happened is slowly being lost in mountain fog."

Gold Diggers

Barring the discovery of some forgotten document it is unlikely that the fog will clear. Cryptozoologists have picked over Beck's accounts for clues about the creature's anatomy and behavior, noted the story's contradictions and inconsistencies, and almost unanimously "ignored the paranormal stuff." Beck, a Spiritualist influenced by esoteric schools of thought, was just as removed from certain ideas as the most scientific Bigfoot hunter, and, in the end, neither the mystic nor the cryptozoologists recognized that *I Fought the Apemen* is a magical treasure-hunting story.

There is a long history of magical treasure hunting in America. It was widely believed that the country was peppered with pirates' gold, misers' hoards, and lost mines, that Indian graves were filled with valuables, and gnomes collected enormous stockpiles of gold and gems in subterranean caves. The notebook of one eighteenth-century money-digger lists the locations of dozens of treasures ("Mrs. Downing of Wair Informs that there is a mine of silver at ye flat rock on Coy's hill in Brookfield"), and places like Bristol Notch, Vermont, were "honeycombed with holes a few feet in depth, where generations of money-diggers have worked their superstitious energies"[44] searching for gold stolen from a Spanish galleon.

On July 20, 1822, the *Lycoming Gazette* (Williamsport, Pennsylvania) reported, "We could name if we pleased five hundred respectable men who do, in the simplicity and sincerity of their hearts, verily believe that immense treasures lie concealed in the Green Mountains; many of whom have been, for a number of years, most industriously and perseveringly engaged in digging it up." Moreover, the article encouraged readers to take up "the mineral [divining] rod and discover a fortune," which leads to the *other* popular belief underpinning magical treasure hunting: that occult methods for finding it worked.

They involved spell casting, nocturnal ceremonies, and communicating with spirits, but despite its resemblance to witchcraft (and even grave robbing), magical treasure hunting was not beyond the pale. It may not have been discussed in polite company, but treasure hunting experienced several waves of popularity during which unknown numbers of citizens were slipping out after dark carrying shovels, swords, and spell books.

The actual money-digging process could be simple or elaborate, but the first step consisted of figuring out where to dig. It might be revealed in dreams, or by a ghost ("'Raise this rock,' said a voice . . . the young man worked most of the night [and] [u]nder it, in old coins, he found money enough to last him the rest of his life").[45] Legends like the story about Spanish gold at Bristol Notch provide a general idea where to look, but some form of magic, such as dowsing, was needed to find to find the precise location.

Dowsing was a popular form of divination that employed rods, pendulums, or other devices colloquially known as "doodlebugs" that signaled the presence of hidden treasure. An Indiana farmer named Wait, for example, used a pendulum weighted with a "mineral ball" that revolved when it was over precious metals, but there were more exotic methods, such as the "peep stones" or "seer stones" employed by the Mormon prophet Joseph Smith Jr. As a young man he used them to see underground treasures just as he later used the holy seer stones, Urim and Thummim, to translate the

Golden Plates into the *Book of Mormon*. Some money-diggers hired diviners like Smith or practiced magic themselves.

Necromancy, the conjuring and questioning of spirits, was the most effective way to discover and secure treasure. "Spells and incantations" with power over spirits is doubly necessary, "first to call up a spirit who shall disclose the right spot and second, to control the demon who keeps the hoard."[46] The "demon" is the spirit that stands guard and must be restrained from attacking the men or moving the treasure out of reach.

When the right location was found, some money-diggers drove an iron spear into the ground to "pin" it in place, while others practiced elaborate rituals. In "A method to Tak [*sic*] up hid Treasure," Silas Hamilton, the enthusiastic hunter whose notebook listed the local buried treasures, described a way of laying out a magic circle that kept the gold in place:

> Tak Nine Steel Rods about ten or twelve Inches in Length Sharp or Piked to Perce in to the Erth, and let them be Besmeared with fresh blood from a hen mixed with hog-dung. Then mak two Surkels Round the hid Treasure one of Sd Surkels a Little Larger in Surcumference than the hid Treasure lays in the Erth the other Surkel Sum Larger still, and as the hid treasure is wont to move to North or South East or west Place your Rods as is Discribed on the other sid of this leaf. [The other side of the page shows the rods laid out in a wheel-shaped pattern.][47]

Many treasure hunters used a ritual sword or dagger to scratch a magic circle into the ground around the area to be excavated, then cast a spell. It might include hymns, Bible readings, or animal sacrifices, but "[s]hould someone carelessly mutter or curse," the enchantment would be broken, and "the treasure guardians could penetrate the circle or carry the treasure through the earth."[48] Digging was done in perfect silence and as the men worked, spirits attempted to confuse and frighten them with phantom storms, fires, ghosts, demons, and monsters.

It must have been unnerving work, scooping dirt out of a dark hole in the middle of the night while a shrieking corpse or giant black pig stalked the outer perimeter of the magic circle, and someone invariably spoke or, more likely, swore whereupon the unprotected diggers ran for their lives, arriving home empty-handed and, in some cases, with their hair turned white from terror. What frightened them?

Most treasure guardians were spirits of the dead. The ghost of the treasure's former owner might stand guard, or, in the case of piratical booty, a member of the burying party or other unfortunate was killed for the purpose (these ghosts seem to have been especially angry). There were phantom animals as well, including fiery-eyed dogs and cats, wild horses, and diabolical livestock. A talking toad threatened to murder treasure hunters at Niagara County, New York, while reptiles, particularly snakes, recall the ancient role of dragons as guardians of the Golden Fleece and other treasures. Snakes also represent Satan, and riches acquired through sin and bloodshed, then hidden within the earth, tended to attract infernal attention.

Five hundred little devils watched over a hoard of silver buried in Safe Harbor, Pennsylvania, and a treasure hunter digging near Dighton Rock, a boulder covered with mysterious carvings at Berkley, Massachusetts, saw "the devil, equipped with all his paraphernalia of tail and horns and cloven hoof, mocking and laughing at him."[49]

There were also beings intimately connected to the Earth, including dwarfish elemental gnomes and gigantic children of the goddess Gaia, which, "[b]ecause of their size and strength . . . made formidable guardians."[50] Joseph Smith Jr. reportedly saw a group of money-diggers routed by a giant standing eight or nine feet tall, and Mr. Wait had an even more alarming encounter. While excavating a hole, he looked up and "beheld a huge millstone suspended above him by a thread, and a giant negro standing by with scissors ready to cut the thread and cause the stone to fall upon him."[51]

Wait survived the millstone (as well as a phantom flood and spectral wild horses), and when he died around 1900, an attempt was made to overturn his will based "largely on the fact that the testator . . . had . . . been imbued with the belief that he possessed the power to locate hidden treasure."[52] The court did not consider magical treasure hunting a sufficient reason to overturn the will, but the case of *Wait v. Westfall* demonstrates how the rational, more or less scientific, worldview that came to dominate public life during the nineteenth century had turned a once-popular pastime into evidence of incompetence or insanity.

While powwow doctors might have been curing hexed cattle in Pennsylvania, root magic flourished in the South, and a vampire was killed at Rhode Island in 1892, such activities were increasingly regarded as the eccentric behavior of superstitious provincials.

Stories about pirate's gold and lost mines are still told, of course, and there is no shortage of hopeful fortune hunters searching for them, but at some point the use of rituals and spells vanished in the United States. What might its adepts, men like Silas Hamilton, Joseph Smith Jr., and Mr. Wait, have made of *I Fought the Apemen of Mt. St. Helens*? Would they recognize the events of 1924 as something akin to their experiences?

The Secret of Ape Canyon

At first reading, Beck's account seems remote from the world of grimoires and buried doubloons. He does not mention any legends about lost mines or hidden gold at Mt. St. Helens, not even a rumor of the sort mentioned by Albert Ostman (discussed shortly). On July 16, 1924, however, the *Seattle Daily Times* reported that "[i]n the vicinity" of the Vander White mine was "a fable of a wonderfully wealthy gold deposit . . .

worked by Yakima Indians." These "pioneer reminiscences" described "Indians bringing great quantities of gold from these mountains and then the supply ceasing when several Indians were killed mysteriously."

Beck's account contains little in the way of folklore or superstition, and there is nothing to suggest that he was familiar with ritual magic, yet Spiritualism was not as removed from sorcery as its adherents claimed. Skeptics thought fraud and credulity explained the phenomena, but others accepted the manifestations as real, if not new. For them it was a revival of necromancy, literally "corpse divining," the ancient form of sorcery used by the Witch of Endor to raise the spirit of Samuel for King Saul (1 Samuel 28).

How the witch went about it is unknown, but the Greek enchantress Circe had a method that involved prayers to the dead and a freshly dug trench filled with honey, milk, wine, and the blood of a ram and ewe, a mixture that gave spirits the strength to speak. Later techniques were more gruesome.

Necromancy was practiced in graveyards at night by the light of lamps that burned human fat and had a piece of shroud for a wick. Practitioners drew magical circles on the ground, made sacrifices, and dug up fresh corpses for rituals whose resemblance to magical treasure hunting is not coincidental, for necromancy was often used to find gold. The advent of Spiritualism, however, rendered such grotesque practices obsolete.

Séances made "communicating with the dead at once

easy, practical, and comfortable. This was the method truly suited to our habits and the refinement of our civilization, and there is no need whatever to go into cemeteries . . . in short, the necromantic craft of the witch has been advantageously replaced by spiritualism."[53]

One important difference between the miners' method of searching for gold and traditional magic was the latter's use of magical spells to shield participants from hostile spirits and protection that was lost if someone spoke. Beck never says that the men thought they were shielded by Spiritualism, or, if they did, that it depended on keeping silent; yet consider events leading up to the discovery of the mine.

The Great Spirit presumably shot the phantom arrow into the sky that led the men on a four-day trek over difficult terrain. Beck does not record anything being said during that time, not until Marion Smith cursed the Great Spirit, whereupon they were told, "[Y]ou will be shown where there is gold, but it is not given you." Smith had broken the spell, allowing guardian spirits to move the "buried treasure" out of the hunters' reach, and lost the miners' equivalent of "magical protection."

> For six years all had been peaceful . . . *and an aura of good or spiritual power surrounded us* . . . But one of us had lost his temper and denounced the spirit leading us a liar, from that time on a quiet apprehensiveness settled over us. We continued working our claim, but down deep we felt it would avail to no good end.[54] [my italics]

Someone remarked, "We just as well pack up and go home," and old-fashioned treasure hunters like Hamilton or Wait would have agreed.

While most traditional treasure hunts seem to have taken place in the course of a single night, events at Ape Canyon unfolded at a leisurely pace. The miners worked for two fruitless years before giants drove them from the mountains, which raises the question of why they were attacked at all. There was no headlong flight from the mountains, but two years of fruitless work before giants drove them away, which raises the question of why they were attacked at all.

Fred Beck believed it was revenge for shooting the ape-man, but what if the "good assay" was accurate and the miners were, as they believed, on the verge of discovering gold? That is when the spirits manifested and drove away the Spiritualists with the same fury visited on their spell-casting predecessors, and leaving them just as empty-handed. Beck wrote, "the fact is that we never took any [gold] out. A few nuggets was the only gold I ever obtained, and they were found in different locations."[55]

The idea that Ape Canyon is a magical treasure-hunting story, and Bigfoot are guarding hidden gold, may seem improbable, but, like traditional earth spirits, Sasquatch are enormous and primitive, throw stones like giants, and are associated with the underground knocking noises characteristic of gnomes (and responsible for the regional name "tommyknockers"); in some certain alternative-reality circles ape-men are also believed to mine gold for aliens, another gnomish trait. Then there is the other classic Bigfoot incident that occurred during the summer of 1924.

Albert Ostman was camping in the wilderness of coastal British Columbia's Toba Inlet when he was carried off and held captive by a family of Sasquatch for six days. Ostman escaped and kept the incident to himself until 1957, when he told the story in an official affidavit and swore an oath to its truth.

Experts studied the account, evaluating the description of the creatures' anatomy, rudimentary language, and technology, and even the amount of time they spent gathering edible plants and whether its nutritional value was adequate to sustain primates of their alleged size. Ivan Sanderson's interview with Albert Ostman concentrated on "certain zoological or anthropological details" and the questions were loaded "with snares and abstruse technical catches . . . ," yet for all this careful investigation, one point is passed over without comment: Ostman's reason for being at the Toba Inlet.[56] "There was allegedly a lost gold mine thereabouts and he decided to take a crack at finding it."[57] Like the miners at Ape Canyon, he might have succeeded had a group of Bigfoot not intervened.

Beings of Earth

In some respects, Sasquatch resemble treasure guardians. Like giants of folklore and mythology, they are enormous, throw stones, live in wildernesses, and are mixtures of animal and human traits. This hybrid quality has been characteristic of giants since the earliest times, with the "earth-born" serpent-legged Gigantes of classical mythology and the hair-covered wodewoses of medieval folklore; it continues today in the belief that contemporary giants are "ape-men." The similarities between Sasquatch and gnomes are less obvious.

Since miners work underground and are in contact with valuable mineral deposits, they are among those most likely to encounter gnomes: elemental spirits that appear as small, dark, malformed men dressed as miners, who are seldom seen but can be heard "knocking and hammering as if three or four smiths were at work . . ." Fred Beck and his party heard subterranean noises at Mt. St. Helens:

> . . . the same thudding, hallow thumping noise we heard at night preceding the attack, we also had heard in broad daylight, although not nearly so loud . . . like there's a hollow drum in the earth somewhere and something is hitting it.[58]

He offers no explanations for the sounds, but decades later, Jack "Kewaunee" Lapseritis, who believes Bigfoot are an alien race of wise, interdimensional nature spirits, experienced something comparable at a campsite on Oregon's Cascade Mountains:

> "Errr-rump, errr-rump, errrrr-rump," an eerie mechanical sound had begun . . . like that of a pumping action with a generator slipping its gears. But what was it? The muffled grinding of gears seemed to be coming from within the earth![59]

Lapseritis implies that the "errr-rumping" comes from a subterranean facility operated by aliens and guarded by Sasquatch. That repetitive underground noises should occur in what are nominally Bigfoot cases suggests some kind of affinity between ape-men and gnomes that is realized in alternative-reality circles.

Lyle Vann, Director of the Arizona Bigfoot Center, also believes ape-men are associated with aliens, but that the Sasquatch are mining gold for extraterrestrials who use it in the electronics of their spaceships. "The creatures are nocturnal. They live in subterranean caves. The aliens use ape-men for mining because they are strong, gentle creatures."[60] (Mining even explains Bigfoot's odor. "'Many people think Bigfoot smells—that he has a bad smell,' Vann said. 'That's not the case in Arizona. The reason is because there is not a lot of sulfur in the ground here. In California, there's a lot of sulfur underground and it gets into the Bigfoot's coat because Bigfoot lives underground. That is what makes them smell.'")[61]

While Vann's ape-men have gnomish habits and occupations, the situation is reversed in a tale from the Sierra Madres in which a gnomelike child, a "hunchbacked dwarf" employed in a mine, is transformed into a treasure-guarding "Sasquatch."

> The story is that when Mexico was first settled by the Spaniards this mine was worked by the natives, and when it was discovered how rich it was the invaders ruthlessly slaughtered every person whom they found working in the place except a lad who was employed carrying water to the miners. He fled at the approach of the Spaniards and saved his life. This boy was a hunchbacked dwarf, and when he found that all his friends and relatives had been murdered he took a horrible oath of revenge, selling his soul to the evil one for the ability to avenge himself. He was given the power to bring destruction upon any one who went into the mine to work, and it is this, which has brought destruction to those who have attempted to get the rich ore from the demon's mine. The story had its origins centuries ago, but there is not a native of Chihuahua who does not have implicit faith in it. They still refuse steadily to work in the mine and tell of many people who have met horrible deaths in the pit.
>
> The demon is said to resemble a huge ape, with hairy body and long powerful arms. It is misshapen, and with deep sunken eyes is seen peering around a corner of the shaft just before it wreaks its vengeance upon the men who are toiling in the rocks and dirt.[62]

The illustration shows three miners dropping tools and fleeing a Bigfoot-like "demon."

Apparently earth-elementals in the shape of ape-men were driving off treasure hunters long before Beck's party escaped in Marion Smith's Ford. It was at Ape Canyon, however, that the ancient art of magical treasure hunting intersected with the aspiring science of cryptozoology and began a long, uncomfortable association in the pages of *I Fought the Apemen.*

Before we conclude this perhaps overlong discussion about monsters guarding buried treasure, there are other places where this old idea might apply.

Mound Monsters

In 1989–1990, writer and researcher Linda Godfrey was a reporter covering sightings of a werewolflike creature on a stretch of road at Elkhorn, Wisconsin. She christened it "the Beast of Bray Road" and went on to collect historical and contemporary eyewitness descriptions of bipedal wolves, "dog-men," and four-footed "hell hounds" seen throughout the upper Midwest. A map was created showing the location of each encounter, and it led to an unexpected connection.

Godfrey was reading *Indian Mounds of Wisconsin*, by Robert A. Birmingham and Leslie E. Eisenberg (Madison: University of Wisconsin Press, 2000), when she saw a map showing the locations of "effigy mounds," ancient earthworks laid out in the shapes of animals, men, and spirits, that caused "a few dozen lightbulbs" to go off in her head.

> Their map of Wisconsin shows major groupings of animal effigy mounds, with different types represented by tiny symbols. It suddenly occurred to me that the placement of the symbols . . . corresponded very closely to a map I had made showing the main concentration of Manwolf sightings around the state!
>
> I made a transparency of my map, sized to fit the one in the book and voila, the connection was undeniable. I couldn't place sightings to exact locations of the mounds, say within a few feet or yards, in every instance, but the distribution of the two phenomena was very much the same . . . some discrepancies should be expected, since the mounds are stationary but the creatures seem to have free ability to roam. Even taking that into consideration, I still think the way the two maps coincide is remarkable. It seems more than mere coincidence, in fact.[63]

She offers several possible explanations. The creatures might be guarding sacred sites, or their tendency to appear near mounds shaped like long-tailed "water panthers" could mean they are water spirits of the Ho-Chunk (Winnebago) tradition. She also suggests that the mounds were built to *contain* spirits and did so until they "were cut open, plowed under and otherwise desecrated by settlers . . . [whereupon] the guardians may have been set free. That would explain the proximity of these creatures to the mound areas, as well as why it was so important to place mounds everywhere and go to such lengths in their construction and design."[64]

To an old-time magical treasure hunter, however, the reason would be obvious: wolf and dog monsters are standing guard over valuables buried inside the mounds The association between apparitions and hidden wealth survived well into the twentieth century, so when a woman in Sandfly, Georgia, encountered a gnome complete with "a lill tin lamp" on his head "wut gleamed in duh dahk," the experience was frightening, yet easily explained, for "[d]ey say he's comin roun cuz deah's *buried treasure* neah yuh."[65] If the Americans that settled Wisconsin in the early nineteenth century had monster sightings like those collected by Godfrey it may explain why so much treasure hunting went on in the mounds.

Before chasing that idea down a rabbit hole, however, it is better to return to Ape Canyon.

Giants in the Woods and Imagination

The attack on the miners' cabin was not the only strange incident at Ape Canyon. Twenty-six years later, in 1950, an experienced mountaineer and skier named Jim Carter vanished, leaving a ski trail that suggested he was desperately trying to escape from *something* and raising suspicions that "the mountain devils got him."[66] Thirty years after that, on May 18, 1980, Mt. St. Helens exploded.

It was a monstrous eruption; a vast swath of countryside was pulverized, forests flattened, lakes emptied, and surrounding areas buried under millions of tons of volcanic ash. Ape Canyon lay outside the path of direct destruction, but melting snow created a torrent of mud and debris that flooded the canyon, carried off the forest, and scoured away any traces of the miners' presence that might have survived the intervening years (though recent investigations have discovered possible fragments of their cabin). Rumors claimed that Bigfoot corpses were found during the cleanup and that they were hastily burned or whisked away, like crashed flying saucers.

As an historical incident, Ape Canyon is a fading oddity. Most of Beck's account is unpalatable to cryptozoologists, while his belief in the spiritual inferiority of ape-men does not appeal to mystics that want their Bigfoot to be wise, magical, and ecologically concerned. With no group claiming that their interpretation of *I Fought the Apemen* is correct, it can be approached without preconceptions. The magical treasure hunt interpretation is consistent with the story's contents and changes it from something at the fringe of cryptozoology literature to a fairly representative example of buried-treasure lore. In fact, it points to another way of understanding Ape Canyon, since

> the basis for such legendary quests [treasure hunts] may lie in symbolic traditions of late antiquity . . . in which "treasures" stood for specific attainments sought on the path to wisdom and knowledge. Guardians block access to these inner treasures and can be commanded only by those who possess secret passwords and geometrical symbols . . . Later traditions may be seen as literalizations of Gnostic doctrine by those with no understanding of its symbolic significance: the treasures become "real" hoards, but access to them continues to depend upon knowing the proper magic words and geometric forms.[67]

From this perspective, the search for gold in *I Fought the Apemen* becomes a metaphor for seeking wisdom. The creatures represent what is primitive in human nature and, because the miners do not master those aspects of themselves, they fail to attain knowledge. This idea can be applied to Bigfoot hunting in general, which then becomes a process for subduing the ape-man in oneself in order to subdue the ape-man in the woods. Perhaps that is why Fred Beck, who did not believe that Sasquatch could be caught or killed, thought that searching for them brought one to the "gates of psychicism." On a more prosaic level, connecting monsters and hidden treasure suggests that a really thorough Bigfoot hunter's equipment should include a metal detector and a shovel.

I Fought the Apemen of Mt. St. Helens repays close reading. Fred Beck concedes that his theories depend on the creatures' existence not being proven, for "[i]f someone captured one, I would have to swallow most of the content of this book." Until that happens, though, Bigfoot will continue to wander through the mountains, forests, and swamps of North America, moving between planes of existence, mining gold for aliens, and transforming those who search for them.

Psychic in the White House

History-minded tourists visit Strasburg, Virginia, for its eighteenth-century inn and Civil War battlefields, but there is a place on North Massanutten Street where cannonballs give way to crystal balls: the Jeane Dixon Museum and Library. Up one flight of stairs stands a monument to the pop prophet's "life as a psychic, devout Catholic, humanitarian, real estate executive, presidential advisor, animal lover and devoted wife."[1]

Four large rooms are furnished with antique furniture, tapestries, stained glass, and statues from the Victorian townhouse that was her Washington, D.C., home, and there is Dixoniana everywhere. Marble-topped tables are covered with scrapbooks full of clippings and photographs, the walls are hung with framed autographed glossies from celebrities and politicians (many of whom she advised), as well as pictures of her telepathic pet, Mike the MagiCat.[2] Dixon's bed, a lacy confection that allegedly belonged to Empress Eugenie of France, has teddy bears and angels dangling from the canopy, and in the room opposite stands a red-lacquered opium-style bed that was a gift from Generalissimo Chiang Kai-Shek. New Age music adds an "ethereal ambiance," but there is little of the unambiguously mystical on display.

Most of this is found in a small section where triffidlike gilded candlesticks sit on a round table surrounded by twelve upright cards that explain Dixon's syncretization of the signs of the zodiac and the Apostles; the shelves are also lined with material including pictures and articles describing her best-known prophecies.[3]

Of the library's many books, there are few about the paranormal, and these are ordinary works on Nostradamus, the Shroud of Turin, and Edgar Cayce; Dixon was not a scholar, and one should not expect anything in the way of grimoires or obscure astrological texts. Her crystal ball is displayed next to an article about health and astrology illustrated by the characters from *The Simpsons*, and considerable space is devoted to cat figurines, silverware, and a formidable collection of Catholic tchotchkes. There are Blessed Virgin Marys of every description, from mass-produced gimcracks to a magnificent painting of Mary, Queen of Heaven, along with several portraits of Dixon.

A formal likeness shows her standing by a fireplace,

looking saintly and slightly undead in what might be a shimmering nurse's uniform, while the rest are saccharine, hallucinatory, or creepy.

The woman behind these images was petite and formidable. She was vain and chatty, had a weakness for funny hats, and started each day facing east while reciting Psalm 23 before attending Mass. Dixon ate little meat, neither smoked nor drank, and according to the museum's owner and her former banker, Leo M. Bernstein: "She was modest. She was ethereal. I didn't look at her like a woman."[4] According to Jeane Dixon, passersby sometimes mistook her for an angel or the Virgin Mary, and she described herself as God's messenger, a prophet in the biblical sense. She also cultivated her legend, deliberately obscuring the real woman until that inconvenient person nearly ceased to exist.

Miss Pinckert and Mrs. Zuercher

Dixon, according to Dixon, was born Jeane Pinckert in 1918, one of seven children of Frank Pinckert and Emma Von Graffee, German immigrants who settled in the town of Medford, Wisconsin. Herr Pinckert had a successful lumber business, and when he retired at age forty-five, the family moved to Santa Rosa, California, where Jeane grew up. She was homeschooled by her parents and a European governess, received voice and polo lessons, and learned riding from American Indians and astrology from a Jesuit priest.

Her unusual talent first appeared as a toddler, when she asked to play with "the letter trimmed in black." Mrs. Pinckert did not have such a letter, but one soon arrived from Germany announcing the death of a relative.[5] The implications of this became clear a few years later when mother and daughter visited a gypsy camp.

The fortune-teller inspected eight-year-old Jeane's palm and was staggered to see a Star of David and a Half Moon, chiromantic configurations that appear once in a millennium and signify greatness as a mystic. The gypsy presented her with a crystal ball, so while other children were playing with toys in the dirt, little Jeane Pinckert was advising celebrities. A few years later, she fell in love with James Lamb Dixon, a much older man, and when he got married, twelve-year-old Jeane's heart was broken.

At various times she considered becoming a nun or an actress before reconciling the two by playing Mary Magdalene in *The Life of Christ* at the Hollywood Bowl; it was around this time that James reentered her life.

He had divorced and began courting Jeane, with Mrs. Pinckert acting as duenna. A pious girl, she naturally had misgivings about marrying the divorced son of a Methodist minister, but they received an ecclesiastical dispensation and were wed; Jeane doesn't mention where or when, only that James gave her a five-carat diamond ring. The couple moved to Washington, D.C., during World War II, and Jeane Dixon, now rich and acquiring influential friends, soon made her mark.[6]

It says something about the times, perhaps, that skeptics who happily pulled apart Dixon's predictions seldom looked into her background, yet the differences between her claims and her history suggest a disconcertingly casual attitude toward truth.[7]

First, she was born in 1904, not 1918. Her siblings confirmed the earlier date, but Jeane insisted on 1918 for reasons unrelated to vanity.[8] Secondly, her real name was Lydia, which she also denied, allowing only that her middle initial was L, and there were ten Pinckert children, not seven. Two became famous in their own right: one an aviatrix and the other a football player, and they are the only ones Dixon ever mentions.

The family lived in Wisconsin until about 1910, then went to Missouri. In 1912, Jeane attended La Grange School outside Carthage, and in 1919, the Pinckerts moved to San Bernardino, California, where they operated a gas station and grocery store. Two years later, Jeane went to work for the Bank of Italy in San Francisco.

If her early life was not a constant round of genteel pursuits, it was unremarkable and might have almost been acceptable had Jeane Dixon not insisted on being a pillar of Roman Catholic propriety. The difficulty was that in 1928 she married a Swiss immigrant named Charles Zuercher and later divorced him (Zuercher died in 1940).[9] Therefore, when James married Jeane (probably in San Diego in 1939), he was around forty-two and owned several Los Angeles car dealerships, while she was an attractive thirty-five-year-old divorcee who worked for him. By subtracting fourteen years from her age and never wavering from it, Jeane—or possibly Lydia—Zuercher was effectively erased.

The Washington Seeress

Washington was full of servicemen during the war, and Jeane volunteered to help entertain them with fortune-telling. She acquired a reputation for accuracy, which led to her doing readings for President Franklin Delano Roosevelt in 1944–1945. Dixon visited the White House twice, discreetly tucking the crystal ball inside the sleeve of her mink, and told the ailing FDR how long he would live, and that America should be fighting with Germany against the Soviet Union. There is no official record of the visits, and staff members did not remember her being there, but Elliott Roosevelt said his father was interested in extrasensory perception (ESP) and had discussed Dixon.[10]

After the war, Jeane lived the life of a Washington matron; she shopped, had her hair done, and attended embassy cocktail parties. James placed a rose on her pillow every morning (an artificial rose is there now), but he was "a stern taskmaster who expected her to be at his beck and call."[11] Despite that, she chose a four-story Victorian row house, which he did not want, as their home, and became secretary-treasurer of James L. Dixon Realtors. Jeane claimed that working in the office was James's way of protecting her from never-ending requests for psychic help, but there were practical reasons for being there.[12]

She had been hired by the San Francisco bank for her "genius at figures and accounting," and presumably continued working in a financial capacity for James's company in California.[13] When it came to business, she was reputedly "tougher than hell, much tougher than her husband really."[14] Despite being employed, Dixon still gave readings at parties, and the 1950s and 1960s would prove to be her most productive period.[15]

During this time she foretold the launching of Sputnik, UN secretary-general Dag Hammarskjöld's plane crash, the deaths of three Apollo astronauts, and much else. She will always be remembered, however, as "the woman who predicted Kennedy's assassination."[16] Space does not permit a fair evaluation of her accuracy, but the JFK prophecy is a good example of how she claimed to experience seeing into the future.

Dixon's countdown to Dallas began in 1952, in Washington, D.C., as she knelt before a statue of the Virgin Mary in the Cathedral of St. Matthew the Apostle. A radiant image of the White House appeared and the number "1960" above it;

dark clouds spread from the numerals and dripped down onto the building like "chocolate frosting on a cake" and a man stood there, "young, tall, and blue-eyed, with a shock of thick brown hair.[17] An inner voice told her that he was a Democrat, and that the President [elected in 1960] would meet with a violent death while in office."[18] Then the vision vanished.

Four years later, *Parade* reported that "for the 1960 election, Mrs. Dixon thinks it will be dominated by labor and won by a Democrat. But he will be assassinated or die in office, 'though not necessarily in his first term.'"[19] When Kennedy was elected in 1960, she saw gloomy clouds and caskets over the White House.

In January 1963, Dixon said Kennedy would be dead before the end of the year.[20] By April, she predicted that he'd be shot, and, in October, that he would probably die in his first term. On November 13, Dixon tried warning Kennedy that he would be assassinated if he traveled "down South."[21] She told radio host Long John Nebel, "Something is going to happen to Jack this week," and, on the twenty-second, allegedly announced, "[T]his is the day it will happen."[22] A shroud she saw over the White House had darkened, and she phoned Nebel to say that the president should not take part in any "political thing" in Dallas; one and a half hours later, Kennedy was dead.[23]

The funeral was held in the cathedral where Jeane first had the fatal vision. She watched on television as the president's casket was placed on a caisson and saw

> John Fitzgerald Kennedy dancing an Irish jig on top of it. He was happy and gay and free! The funeral procession moved slowly down the avenue with the President continuing his merry twirling . . . I saw Uncle Sam raise both his hands, as if pronouncing a benediction, and when I glanced back at the caisson only a fleecy trail of smoke remained where the President had danced.[24]

(Her visions resemble nothing so much as political cartoons and were sometimes criticized for "vulgarity.")[25] Kennedy's death made Dixon's reputation, but other visions augured change for the whole human race.

Jeane was lying in bed in July 1952 when a giant snake coiled itself around her and wordlessly communicated that she must look to the east for "God's wisdom and guidance."[26] Ten years later, another vision explained why.

On the morning of February 5, 1962, she looked out her bedroom window and saw "a bright blue sky over a barren desert." There was a pyramid, and the sun contained the patriarch Joseph, who apparently directed the actions of Queen Nefertiti and her "Pharaoh husband," presumably Akhenaten. They approached carrying a baby wrapped in rags, and the scene changed; the infant had become a man with a cross in the air above him that "dripped over the earth." People of every race and religion surrounded him "in worshipful adoration" and Jeane joined them till the vision ended, whereupon she presumably went downstairs and ate breakfast.[27]

Dixon believed that a descendant of the Egyptian royal couple was born that day to poor parents in the Middle East and that the "Child of the East" would unite humankind under a new form of Christianity before the end of the century. Several Christian writers saw the snake as Satan and the child as the Antichrist and concluded that "the devil is using her [Dixon] to deceive the multitudes and to prepare them to receive the great delusion which is to come . . ."[28] By 1969, she had taken up this interpretation, possibly to deflect criticism, or having concluded that the Child of the East was not a "revelation."

The Divining Mrs. D

Jeane Dixon's revelations were her most important psychic experiences. They communicated the will of God and were distinguished by the clarity of their meaning, an accompanying sense of euphoria, and the inevitability of their outcome. Ordinary visions, such as those she experienced spontaneously, or while meditating or crystal gazing, were more ambiguous. Once, while attending a wedding, Dixon saw coffins behind the bride and groom and assumed the worst, yet it was the best man and groom's brother who died.

Visions could be misinterpreted, but she claimed the predictions were correct *when they were made*, "because she got

[them] . . . through mental telepathy. 'This is the way people feel right now,' she said. But, if they should change their minds, then that would change the answer."[29] Presumably, if a general was planning an invasion, Dixon would correctly predict that war was imminent; if he changed his mind and there was no war, that didn't make her wrong.

In addition to visions and crystal gazing, Jeane would become a famous astrologer, casting horoscopes psychically rather than by doing calculations. She disapproved of mediumistic practices and does not mention Tarot, but Dixon sometimes asked people to shuffle a pack of ordinary playing cards (another gift from the gypsy fortune-teller) before doing a reading; it helped her tune in to their vibration. One witness reported that Jeane correctly diagnosed an illness by looking at a photograph; another said she cured his warts.

Though Dixon does not seem to have been particularly interested in numerology, her calendar was marked with good and bad days; five, seven, and nine were the best numbers, four and eight the worst. She might have done this for Nancy Reagan as well; chief of staff Donald Regan reported that the First Lady prepared a calendar for the president in which "[n]umerals were highlighted in green ink for good days, red ink for bad days and yellow ink for 'iffy' days . . ."[30] And Dixon never stopped making predictions.

Journalist Martha Rountree was told that she would not

live in her new house, and it burned down before she could move in. Jeane saw Marilyn Monroe committing suicide, Red China invading the Soviet Union, and giant squid becoming "an inexpensive and very healthy food source."[31] One vision showed Negroes "being pushed by an underground force [Communists]" to seek "equal powers and jobs before they have the intellectual capacity and understanding to accept equal responsibility," which makes uncomfortable reading for several reasons.[32]

Making a Prophet

Newspaper columnist Ruth Montgomery worked with Dixon to write a book about her life and predictions called *A Gift of Prophecy: The Phenomenal Jeane Dixon* (1965), which sold a remarkable three million copies and made Jeane a national figure.

Dixon became a regular on television and radio as well as a popular lecturer; at one point a Gallup poll named her the eleventh most admired woman in America. Supermarket tabloids carried annual New Year's predictions, Jeane's astrology column was syndicated, and she hired ghostwriters to produce books on everything from Jesus to cooking based on horoscope; ("I'm a Capricorn, my astrological foods . . . are beets, saffron, quince, and barley"); Ruth Montgomery was dropped.[33]

Apart from writing, Jeane also read excerpts from *A Gift of Prophecy* on a forty-five-rpm record and supplied predictions for the world's first "Horoscopes by Phone." In 1968, Milton Bradley put out Jeane Dixon's Game of Destiny: A Card Game of Numerology and Astrology with a message on the box informing purchasers that: "All royalties received by Jeane Dixon from this game will go to the Children to Children Foundation—a medical hospital for children all over the world."

This wasn't quite accurate. Dixon created Children to Children so that money from her psychic ventures would go to charity, yet the foundation's mission was vague and its ultimate goal was creating the Jeane Dixon Medical Center. Plans called for a gigantic, wheel-shaped complex with an airstrip, petting zoo, and eternal flame, but a scale model was all that was built, and the organization was run in an inept, self-serving way that produced the one real scandal of Dixon's career.[34]

Two articles in the March 1970 issue of the *Washingtonian* reported that $5,000 was collected between June 1967 and May 1972, of which 19 percent went to charitable causes, and the rest to pay salaries and publicize Dixon. She tried intimidating the *Washingtonian*'s editor with her connections ("I know people who control billions, not millions"), threatened them with a $5,000,000 libel suit, and brought one for $1,000,000 that was dismissed.[35] The bad publicity soon faded, though, and she remained synonymous with precognition, not misappropriation.

As the country's best-known psychic, Dixon also became the subject of numerous urban legends. She repeatedly had to deny predicting massacres on college campuses, earthquakes, and that all women with pierced ears would die on June 4, 1968. Her name was also a shorthand way of referring to psychic predictions in general or, in one case, how people respond to alleged predictions.

Mathematics professor John Allen Paulos described a phenomenon that he christened "the Jeane Dixon Effect," arguing that belief in prophecy occurs when "relatively few correct predictions are heralded and therefore widely remembered, while the much more numerous incorrect predictions are conveniently forgotten or de-emphasized."[36] The lady herself, however, was not concerned with mathematicians but subversives.

Jeane and the G-Men

The Dixons' FBI file chronicles their long relationship with the Federal Bureau of Investigation and reveals an eagerness on her part to act as a propagandist.

James and Jeane knew J. Edgar Hoover socially, and the Bureau's Washington field office "had liaison with the James

L Dixon Company, which . . . rented property to Soviet-bloc personnel." In 1966, Jeane asked to be "furnished material by the Bureau on an extremely confidential basis, which she might utilize in her speeches," presenting it "in such a manner that it cannot be attributed to the FBI."[37] Hoover approved the request and provided "public source background information" about groups involved in campus disturbances.[38] Four years later, she wrote to the FBI that one of her tenants was operating "some sort of Communistic Press," then phoned a few days after that, fearing for her safety.[39] This became a pattern.

Jeane was scheduled to speak in Greenwood, Mississippi, on January 22, 1970, when a telegram arrived from the "Greenwood movement" informing her that the audience would be segregated and asking for "verification of delivery" of the message. She interpreted this as a threat and once again asked the FBI for protection. They suggested she contact the Greenwood police department.[40]

The file also contains information about an attempt at blackmailing Dixon, newspaper clippings about her predictions with discussions and comments by agents, material from the Children to Children Foundation, and suggestions from concerned citizens who believed "this gal [Dixon] should be checked on."[41] (There is also a letter to Louisiana's Senator Hale Boggs that explains how the Gideon Bible's "daily Bible reading calendar" links the assassinations of

John F. and Robert F. Kennedy, the Rosicrucians, the Ku Klux Klan, the Masons, the Mafia, and Charlie Brown (Snoopy's owner). Dixon is mentioned repeatedly since she has "marked all of our Democrat Leaders [*sic*] for murder or bodily harm." There are also references to a manuscript titled "PREMEDITATED MURDER BY PROPHECY, and [*sic*] Jeane L. Dixon, an alleged 'divine' prophetess plays a major role."[42] The document is not included, but a year later, Senator Boggs's plane vanished over Alaska. Coincidence?)

Senior Seer

James died in 1984, but Dixon kept working, supporting conservative causes, and advising the rich and powerful. In 1988, it was learned that Nancy Reagan had often consulted her, but by then the First Lady had switched to astrologer Joan Quigley, possibly because Dixon's powers seemed to diminish with age.[43]

Jeane Dixon died of heart failure in 1997 and her ashes were scattered over Mt. Rainier—but the story was not over.

After the 9/11 attacks, government terrorism archives were reviewed and it was discovered that President Richard M. Nixon had met with Dixon following the massacre of Israeli athletes at the 1972 Munich Olympics. She predicted that Palestinian radicals would soon be murdering prominent American Jews, and Nixon set up a short-lived "counterterrorism committee."[44] It was an odd episode, even by the standards of the Nixon administration.

An American Prophet

Radio host Barry Farber once said: "Keeping up with Jeane Dixon is like trying to nail a custard pie to the wall!"[45] Summarizing her life is no less difficult.

Of the countless predictions she made, some were accurate, detailed, and corroborated by witnesses.[46] Parapsychologists never tested her abilities—God's messenger doesn't fool around with Zener cards—but describing her power in religious terms meant Dixon had to be saintly, so she invented, and maintained, an appropriate biography. As the unthreatening and "very reputable" face of phenomena that many regard with suspicion, Dixon was the Billy Graham of ESP, providing supernatural help to the elite while being admired by the general public.[47]

At a time when values were under attack, she defended patriotism, self-reliance, and religion, identifying the source of social upheavals in the "organizational geniuses of Russia" rather than failures of civil rights or the war in Vietnam.[48] Even the trauma of a presidential assassination was turned into a celebration and this spoke to a certain innate optimism, for while Dixon often predicted horrors, in the end humankind would transcend its differences and create a utopia.

Whatever Jeane Dixon's shortcomings as a person or prophet, she holds a unique place in American history as the country's only national psychic.

The Jeane Dixon Museum and Library is gone. Like so many small museums, it did not survive its founder, Leo M. Bernstein, who died in August 2008. The contents were eventually packed into five hundred boxes, loaded into five moving vans, and transported to an auction house at Chevy Chase, Maryland, where they were put on display to potential buyers.

Dixon's estate went under the gavel on July 26, 2009, and though she had been dead twelve years, her appeal proved durable. It was standing room only on the auction house floor, with offers coming in via telephone and the Internet from across the country, as well as Russia, England, and Australia. Some lots were bargains; Mike the MagiCat's wardrobe "including tuxedo, overalls, kilt and beret" sold for only $60. The antique furniture, paintings, and décor brought predictably high prices, but the premier item was Jeane Dixon's crystal ball.

People came to see the sphere, just four inches in diameter, which stood on a "separate gilt-metal stand cast as four figural caryatids" and sold for $11,950. It was the third-highest price realized that day (a "secondary crystal ball" brought in a respectable $2,800), with the overall gross exceeding all expectations, reaching $312,349.[49]

If the results happened to reach the Other Side, a petite spirit with a genius for accounting and an Adolfo hat no doubt smiled.

Ku Klux Klowns

One morning in 1981, two little girls were walking down the street of a Midwestern city, so deep in conversation that they did not notice the yellow van following them. It picked up speed, got ahead of the pair, and pulled over to the curb, where the vehicle sat idling. Older boys called vans like that "shaggin' wagons" and though the girls were vague on specifics (did "shaggin'" refer to shag carpeting?), the term provoked embarrassed giggles. Despite its bright color, they paid no attention to this one until the passenger-side window rolled down and a white-gloved hand beckoned to them.

The hand was attached to a clown. He had a chalk-white face and round red nose, with a grin painted across his mouth, and an oversized wig of curly red hair. There was a miniature derby perched on top and the clown tipped it courteously in the girls' direction—then said that he and his companions (two more grease-painted faces appeared at the window) were lost; would the girls get into the van and help them find the circus? The clowns had more candy than they could possibly eat and would give it to them. Though young, the girls were not naïve; they wanted to see the candy first.

The van's side panel slid open with a metallic rumble and a big clown in a red polka-dotted suit climbed out; there were neither lollipops nor candy bars in his hand, but a long-bladed carving knife. The girls shrieked and sprinted away with the clown in pursuit.

While this scene is imaginary, it dramatizes some of the real encounters with unfunny clowns that children across America claimed to be having at the beginning of the 1980s.

In May 1981, the Fortean researcher and writer Loren Coleman was living at Cambridge, when the first reports came in of clowns trying to lure kids into their van in Brookline, Boston, and soon from East Boston, Charlestown, Cambridge, Canton, Randolph, and other cities near Boston. When the reports jumped to include Rhode Island as well, Coleman decided to sweep his network and wrote to all of his American associates and informants to learn if there was similar activity in their areas. He was shocked and startled by what he found—which was being totally ignored by the national media. The eastern United States was under a full-scale invasion of "Phantom Clowns," a phrase he decided to coin to capture the essence of them.[1]

Coleman describes what happened in his 1983 book, *Mysterious America*; it is summarized here along with information on additional sources):

- April 26–May 2, Boston, Massachusetts: Reports were made of "adults dressed as clowns . . . bothering children to and from school." Parents were told to advise children "that they must stay away from strangers, especially ones dressed as clowns."[2]

- May 5, Brookline, Massachusetts: Two clowns were reported driving an older-model black van, with ladders on its side, no hubcaps, and a broken headlight. They tried luring children inside with candy and were sighted near an elementary school.

- May 6, Boston again: Clowns in a black van were harassing children at a park and a school; one clown was reported to be naked from the waist down.

- May 8: There were more sightings of clowns-in-vans in East Boston, Charlestown, Cambridge, Canton, Randolph, and other cities nearby. "Police were stopping vehicles with clowns delivering birthday greetings and 'clown-a-grams,' but no child molesters were arrested."[3]

- Children at Providence, Rhode Island, begin telling psychiatric social workers about clowns.

- May 10–16, Kansas City, Kansas: Children claimed that a white-faced clown with a sword ordered them into a yellow van. They ran away and the clown chased them.[4]

- May 22, Kansas City, Missouri: The mother of two sisters, age six and seven, was watching them walk to the school bus stop, when a yellow van pulled up. The driver apparently spoke to the girls, who ran home screaming, and the vehicle took off. They said that "a dark–haired man . . . wearing a clown outfit and . . . a painted face 'with red polka dots' . . ." had brandished a knife and ordered them inside.[5] This may be the incident a later article describes as "a confirmed sighting from at least one adult in a predominantly black neighborhood in Kansas City, MO," which led to the stories "being viewed with some concern."[6] There were also reports from six different elementary schools, with police receiving calls at the rate of "about one a minute."[7] Several clowns driving vans were stopped that turned out to be entertainers heading to parties.

- A clinical psychologist at the Wyandotte Mental Health Center suggested this was a case of "group hysteria," while a newspaper writer dubbed it the "Demon Clown." Our Lady and St. Rose school distributed memos warning parents about a "Killer Clown."[8]

- May 24, Kansas City, Kansas, and Kansas City, Missouri: There were reports of a "garishly painted" van, and LaTanya Johnson, a sixth-grader at Fairfax Elementary School, saw a clown "dressed in a black shirt with a devil on the front. He had candy canes down each side of his pants."[9]

- June 1–6: Rumors circulated in Pittsburgh, Pennsylvania, about a clown hiding in the woods and attempted child abductions by men dressed as Spider-Man, Superman, and a gorilla. A man wearing a rabbit costume and driving a blue van reportedly raped two children; he may have also been spotted going into a tavern or, perhaps, running through a cemetery.

- There were also reports from Omaha, Nebraska, and Denver, Colorado.

Loren Coleman compares the appearance of the clowns to the legend of the Pied Piper of Hamelin, the musical exterminator who cleared the city of rats and then led the children away forever. In both cases, strangers in exotic clothing appear from nowhere and threaten to carry away a community's children. The story of the Pied Piper is often interpreted as a memory of the Children's Crusade of 1212, when religious enthusiasm led to the youth of France and Germany setting out to liberate Jerusalem from the Saracens, with disastrous results. Beyond fears of child abduction, the clowns-in-vans should be considered in relationship to the pedophilia, serial killing, and satanism panic that beset Americans at the end of the twentieth century.

This chapter argues that phantom clowns did not step out of the collective imagination fully formed, and drive off in a fleet of waiting vans, but are a traditional terror required to cope with a new threat, and based, like the Pied Piper of Hamelin, on memories of traumatic experiences.

White-Faced Terrors

The history of clowns-in-vans begins with the demand for labor created by colonizing the New World. After enslaving

Indians proved unsuccessful, Africans were shipped to North America and a system of chattel slavery was created that continued in the South until the end of the Civil War. It was maintained in modified form for another century by oppressive laws and violence that kept former slaves in a position where they could continue to be exploited. Three of the instruments used to control black populations during and after slavery are relevant to this history.

The first was an antebellum form of policing devised to thwart slave rebellions. "Every slave we own is an enemy we harbor," went the ancient Roman proverb, and fear of insurrections haunted Southern landowners.[10] They tried to prevent slaves on different plantations from making coordinated plans by requiring them to have written permission to be abroad at night, a rule enforced by small groups of white men that patrolled the roads. The "patterollers" whipped slaves who did not have a valid pass, chased runaways, broke up meetings, and discouraged nocturnal wandering by dressing as ghosts, wearing "white robes, or sheets, and masks" and using stage props, such as "a rotating false head, which gave the appearance of all-around vision."[11]

Patterolling ended with slavery, but with the war lost, and former slaves acquiring political power under the protection of federal troops, Southern whites embarked on a campaign to restore the old system. Numerous groups emerged to drive out carpetbaggers and Republicans, including paramilitaries like the White League, and clandestine groups called Redcaps, Knights of the White Camellia, and, most important, the Ku Klux Klan.

The latter's name probably derives from the Greek word *kuklos*, "circle," and what began as a fraternal order set up by Confederate veterans in 1865, with all the extravagant titles, ceremonies, and other trappings typical of secret societies, was soon engaged in intimidation backed by horrific violence. Like the patterollers, members of the "Hooded Order" cultivated a supernatural reputation.

White robes and conical hoods came later; the early Klansmen paraded on horseback in bizarre masks, false beards, horns, and peaked hats ("Dr. Avery had on a red gown with a blue face, with red about his mouth, and he had two horns on his cap about a foot long"[12]). They claimed to be the spirits of Southern soldiers killed in battle and would visit black families in order to play gruesome tricks, such as demanding a drink and seeming to swallow bucketfuls of water while emptying it into a concealed rubber bag. Sometimes they extended a skeletal hand to shake, or seemed to remove their own heads. The latter inspired stories about Klansmen being able to disassemble themselves, but they were also said to emerge from the ground at night like cicadas and had an appearance so terrifying that the sight of them could cause pregnant women to have babies that were "a perfect representation of a disguised Ku Klux" (several of these monstrous births were reported in Alabama).[13] What is most relevant to phantom clowns, however, is the identification of the Klan with the medical profession, a belief that came together in the form of *night doctors*.

Night Doctors

In 1838, a Dr. T. Stillman of Charleston, South Carolina, placed an advertisement in the Charleston Mercury, expressing his interest in buying "*fifty negroes*."

> Any person having sick negroes, considered incurable by their respective physicians and wishing to dispose of them, Dr. S. will pay cash for negroes affected with [list of conditions]. The highest cash prize will be paid upon application as above.[14]

Dr. Stillman was interested in performing experiments and testing new drugs, and a system that classified blacks as property denied them "the legal right to refuse to participate."[15] The extent of this sort of experimentation before the Civil War is unknown, but after Emancipation, there were notorious medical studies like the Tuskegee Experiment, which followed the progress of untreated syphilis in black men.[16] Women were sterilized without their knowledge or consent (a "Mississippi appendectomy"), and the general attitude, as expressed to a reporter in 1893, seems to have been that "doctors don't care for us poor black folks. They want us to cut up, but they don't keer for us . . ."[17] Nor did death did mean an end to victimization.

Black cadavers were regularly stolen, preserved in spirits, and shipped to schools across the country. The trade was so regular that instructors had standing orders ("[a] Professor of Anatomy in a New England medical school told me . . . he had an arrangement under which he received in each session a shipment of twelve bodies of Southern Negroes. They came in barrels marked 'turpentine' . . ."[18] From a black perspective, there was often little difference between the KKK and the AMA, and their fears of the profession were embodied in the idea of "night doctors" (also called "slab doctors," "night witches," "Needle Men," *studients*, and "ku klux doctors").

Night doctors were believed to be medical students, doctors, and corpse vendors who went out in "droves" between midnight and dawn, searching for victims. They wore masks, Klan-style hoods, white lab coats, or dark clothes for hiding in the shadows; and haunted the neighborhoods around medical buildings, colleges, and train depots (Union Station in Washington, D.C., was a favorite hunting ground). These places were especially dangerous for those who were fat or had "peculiar physical conformation . . . which renders their dissection of particular interest to medical students"; it was said that "first class hump-backed subjects" worth a reported $150.[19]

When night doctors tried grabbing a person, some fought back; others believed that "shootin' 'em is no good, an' dey turn the edge of a razzar jest like a stone wall," so the best plan was to run.[20] In 1904, a man in Washington, D.C., escaped by jumping off Long Bridge into the Potomac River, though some accounts read like urban legends.[21]

The doctors, it was claimed, used chloroform to capture victims, as well as throwing hypodermics filled with paralyzing drugs ("flying needles") and slapping adhesive plasters over their mouths to stifle cries. Once subdued, they were bound, gagged, blindfolded, and put into a hearselike wagon with rubber wheels, pulled by dark, rubber-shod horses, that quietly trundled captives off to the nearest hospital or college.

Night doctors were "young student doctors" who carried out gruesome medical procedures and experiments on their prisoners, for they "got their experience that way," and then killed them. Victims were hanged from the ceiling, exposing "a laughing nerve on the bottom of the foot. When the nerve was cut the victim laughed and laughed until he laughed himself to death."[22] The incision also drained the blood, and was described in a secondhand account:

> He said he seed 'em ketch a little girl, an' dey put sumpin' nudder yer [pointing to the front and back of his head], an den dey put a band roun' her body to keep de cirklashun from movin', an den dey strung her up, an' she was laughin' all de time, kind o' conjured like. In 'bout five minutes de blood all runned out o' her feet into a bucket, an' den she was toted off to de 'sectin room.'[23]

Blood and fat were used to make medicines. "One old colored woman insisted that she knows the white men make castor oil out of negro blood, and that in slavery times a negro would die before he could take a dose of castor oil."[24]

Belief in night doctors persisted, "at least" into the 1930s, and "disadvantaged people chose to avoid certain cities altogether, certain parts of cities in the daytime (areas adjacent to hospitals), and many avoided traveling at all at night unless accompanied by small groups. Whether fact or simply fear, the night doctor had certainly captured the imagination of the folk."[25] Some doctors (like the grave robbers that supplied anatomy classes) were black; nevertheless, they follow the pattern established by patterollers and the KKK in which roving bands of grotesquely dressed, white-faced men abduct, torture, and kill black people.

Atlanta

Every period has its characteristic anxieties, and during the late 1970s and 1980s, many of these concerned children. Countless numbers were reportedly being abducted by pedophiles or ritually abused at daycare centers by satanic cults; moreover, the country seemed overrun by homicidal maniacs.

Between 1900 and 1959, American police recorded an

average of two serial murder cases per year nationwide. By 1969, authorities were logging six cases per year, a figure that nearly tripled in the 1970s. By 1985, new serial killers were being reported at an average rate of three per month, a rate that remained fairly constant through the 1990s.[26]

Americans developed a horrified fascination with the crimes, but it was a series of child murders in Georgia that produced the mixture of traditional and contemporary fears that became the basis for clowns-in-vans.

From July 1979 to June 1981, dozens of black children and adolescents were murdered in Atlanta. Almost all the victims were male, and many were strangled or suffocated, and their bodies hidden in overgrown areas. Over time the pattern changed and came to include adult men, whose bodies were sometimes dropped into local rivers to wash away physical evidence. This new behavior prompted police to stake out the bridges, and before dawn, on May 22, 1981, police heard a loud splash coming from the Chattahoochee River just as twenty-three-year-old Wayne Bertram Williams was driving slowly across the bridge; two days later, the body of a twenty-seven-year-old man was found downstream, leading to Williams's arrest. He was convicted of murdering two men in 1982 and received consecutive life sentences; police attributed most of the murders to Williams and considered them solved.

That the killer turned out to be black surprised much of the public as well as law enforcement. For two years, conventional wisdom in the black community had been that the Klan or a similar group was responsible—a reasonable assumption at a time when black serial killers were rare and, more to the point, the city had elected its first black mayor. The killing of black children was seen as a means of spreading fear, heightening tensions, and diminishing confidence in the authorities. (There are still those, including Wayne Williams, who claim he was convicted on weak evidence to prevent rioting.) Georgia's former governor, President Jimmy Carter, considered a racial motive likely enough to order the Federal Bureau of Investigation to assist the police task force, and the Georgia Bureau of Investigation (GBI) put alleged Klansmen under surveillance.

This line of inquiry failed to produce convincing results, but the FBI report contains a number of different scenarios describing who might be committing the murders. A section headed "Theory" proposes:

> That the core killings, of children, in Atlanta, are the work of a small, fanatical, right-wing cell (possibly linked with the KKK, American Nazi party, Minutemen, or other right-wing organization).

The "killer group" was estimated to be

> four to five, white males, twenty-five to fourty [*sic*] years old. These would be males in their top years of physical

> condition, powerful enough to overcome the resistance of a child without help.[27]

It goes on to describe how the abductions could be carried out and the sorts of vehicles that might be involved:

> [One] promising type would be a small van of some kind. Not one with a fancy, "Star Wars," paint job (that would attract too much attention) or a window van, but a simple panel van (probably with one way decals on the rear windows). Such a vehicle would draw little attention to itself, and could provide a rolling murder scene (and if the vehicle is carpeted inside, it could account for some of the fibers found on a few of "the bodies").[28]

Civilians were thinking along similar lines. Atlanta's current (2014) mayor, Kasim Reed, was ten years old during the murders and remembers that "[e]verybody was very mindful of vans at that time."[29] Coincidentally, the KKK was also identifying itself with vans through the recruiting slogan, "Get on the Klan Van—Join the Klan Youth Corps."[30]

White racists, however, were not the only possibility. Vans had long been associated with sex and drugs and proved popular with a number of contemporary serial killers, including Ted Bundy, Gerald and Charlene Gallego, Roy Norris and Lawrence Bittaker, and the Chicago Ripper Crew (vehicles with tinted windows or enclosed cargo areas are still called "murder vans").

Other possible killers were a pedophile gang, while Roy Innis, president of the Congress of Racial Equality (CORE), insisted they were ritual murders carried out by white Satanists.[31] The most interesting and revealing suggestion, however, came from comedian-activist Dick Gregory, who thought that Atlanta might be an "experiment."

During a televised interview with the *Detroit Black Journal* in 1981, Gregory stated that sources told him that the victims were strangely mutilated; nine of seventeen bodies had "the tip of their penises . . . missing" and "hypodermic marks on their testicles," while the remaining eight boys were too decomposed to determine if they had been similarly maimed. Gregory, however, claimed that the bodies did not match the missing children, which led him to think that they were alive in a laboratory where scientists were gathering white blood cells from the boys' penises to produce the cancer-fighting drug interferon. Their motive might not be racist in the ordinary sense, but a result of some useful quality present in sickle cell blood. Therefore:

> The "Atlanta Child Murders" were a blind with substitute corpses identified as the victims of a nonexistent serial killer to conceal the experiments. Dick Gregory did not call it a conspiracy and cover-up, but felt that the CIA,

> FBI, National Institute of Health, Centers for Disease Control, and Emory Hospital should not be excluded from the investigation.[32]

In James Baldwin's book-length meditation on the murders, he writes that

> [p]eople found this an appalling suggestion. I did not. I wondered why they did. It was during my lifetime, after all, and in my country, somewhere in a prison in the "American" South, that Black men with syphilis were allowed to die, while being scrutinized.[33]

Though Baldwin considers the "suggestion" plausible in light of the Tuskegee syphilis study, Gregory is describing the murders in terms of night doctors. Unlike Innis's satanists, the "fiendish experiment" hypothesis is based on a widespread tradition, and similar ideas might have enjoyed greater currency than was acknowledged publicly. (Suspicions about white institutions are so deeply rooted that a 1990 poll conducted by the *New York Times*/WCBS-TV News found that "10% of Black Americans thought that the AIDS virus had been created in a laboratory in order to infect Black people. Another 20% believed that it could be true."[34]) In addition to being consistent with existing beliefs, Gregory's ideas also provide a measure of perverse reassurance. Instead of dark, incomprehensible forces at work within the black community, the source of danger is external and has familiar motives: white society's agencies and institutions were once again exploiting black people by taking their blood and using it to make medicine to heal whites.

If rumors about Atlanta involving Klansmen/night doctors and children being abducted in vans were circulating through the black community nationwide, they could have provided the basis for the clowns. When the panics were going on, many assumed that the two were related (Pittsburgh police thought it was "some sort of hysteria perhaps related to child slayings in Atlanta . . . ," but how close a connection existed was not then apparent.[35] Perhaps the unexpected, and seemingly absurd, involvement of clowns proved distracting, and some kind of explanation, however speculative, seems warranted.

Kkklowns

John Wayne Gacy is one possibility. A respectable Chicago contractor, Gacy was a Jaycees Man of the Year who participated in local politics and entertained at charity events dressed as clowns named "Pogo" or "Patches." In December 1978, police discovered that Gacy had also raped, tortured, and murdered more than thirty young men and adolescent boys, burying most of the bodies in a crawl space beneath his suburban ranch house and filling it with the smell of rotting flesh.

Gacy seems like the obvious inspiration for the panic. He was dubbed the "Killer Clown" and the murders received extensive coverage from 1979 to 1980. Gacy was a sexual sadist whose victims were often minors; he owned a black van, and widely reproduced photographs of Pogo and Patches radiate palpable depravity. Nevertheless, his role is probably a secondary, if surprising one (see the following discussion).

Another popular candidate is the shape-shifting, child-eating villain of Stephen King's horror novel *It*, "Pennywise the Dancing Clown." While Pennywise and John Wayne Gacy certainly launched a generation of coulrophobes, King's book did not come out until 1986, and the television dramatization four years after that. Perhaps the explanation does not lie in one clown figure or another but in an accident of language.[36]

The words *Klan* and *clown* are similar (*clown* also sounds like KKK jargon names such as *Kludd*, *Kloran*, and *Kleagle*), and if black communities around the country were discussing the murders as the work of Klansmen driving vans, perhaps children interpreted *Klan* as *clown*. None of the 1981 panics happened in the South, where the KKK was active (few, if any, clown panics have been recorded there), which suggests that clowns-in-vans were created to fill the void somewhere that fear of the Klan existed but the Klan did not.

That kind of situation could conceivably arise when a Southern black population relocates to somewhere like Newark, New Jersey.

Birth of a Notion

If a birthplace for clowns-in-vans exists, then Newark might be where it happened. The city's port and factories attracted black workers from "Maryland, Virginia, the Carolinas, Georgia, and Florida" at the beginning of the twentieth century and, despite the opening of a Klan headquarters on Broad Street in 1921, immigrants from the South kept coming until a majority of residents were black.[37] In 1978, the city also experienced mysterious disappearances.

On August 20, 1978, five adolescent boys, ages sixteen and seventeen, were playing basketball together when they were hired to move boxes. After the job was finished, the five were dropped off at Clinton Avenue, then vanished. Despite years of investigation, and the chief suspect's trial and acquittal in 2011, what happened to them remains unknown. Newark's main disappearance happened eleven months before Atlanta's, and while there is no proof that it inspired rumors about night doctors at work in New Jersey, the earliest report of clowns-in-vans discovered so far comes from Newark during Halloween, 1980.[38]

> Earlier this week, rumors spread throughout Newark, N.J., that a trio disguised as two clowns and a witch were jumping out of a black van and attacking youngsters. The story was that children had been pricked with a needle, kidnapped and harassed. One report had it that witches were jumping out of vans and threatening to turn all the children into frogs.
>
> Newark police said the hysteria may have been related to the mysterious slayings of the children in Atlanta.[39]

The reference to children being "pricked with a needle" appears in no other clown reports and recalls the night doctors' syringes ("Soon as they catch you alone, they'd stick a needle in you that numbs you") and the "hypodermic marks" that Dick Gregory said were on the Atlanta victims' testicles. It also suggests that the story was in a transitional state, a sort of *Archaeopteryx*, displaying traits of both traditional Klan/night doctors and the emerging clowns.[40]

Untethered from their KKK/night doctor origins, clowns ceased to menace the children of a specific community and threatened children in general, making it possible for the story to spread into the larger society and then around the world.

After the nationwide flaps of 1981, reports of clowns-in-vans, or on foot, continued. A partial list of places includes Boston in 1983; Phoenix, Arizona, in 1985; Chicago, Newark, and surrounding cities in 1991; and Sydney and St. Albans, Australia. Clowns were seen in Washington, D.C., and Capitol Heights, Maryland, in 1994, while Latin America experienced prolonged panics.

Clowns have allegedly abducted countless children from Mexico, South America, and Central America for illegal adoption, organ harvesting, or the sex trade; by 1995, it reached the point where "more than 60 clowns" at Tegucigalpa, Honduras, "burned their costumes in a downtown park to protest the kidnapping of children by armed men dressed as clowns."[41]

In the United States, clowns also appeared in Fitchburg, Wisconsin, in 2000, then returned to Chicago in 2008, and outbreaks still occur from time to time.

The witches, superheroes, and other costumed figures—whose many shapes suggest an unsettled aspect of the phenomenon—have disappeared, while different forms have evolved from the original clowns-in-vans. While some are simple variations, such as black clowns, and others that are nearly unrecognizable, like the "Puppet Man" of New South Wales, Australia, who drove a van filled with life-sized animal puppets and attacked two women. The clown's descendants may even include London's "Chelsea Smilers," who were

> a group of Chelsea football fans traveling London in a van with a smiley face painted on the side. They would stop schoolchildren and ask them questions about Chel-

> sea football club. If the children got the questions wrong—perhaps they didn't support Chelsea or, worse, didn't like football—the gang would slice the corners of their mouth . . . then hit the child hard enough to make them scream, which widened their wounds into a "smile."[42]

The combination of van, child victims, and exaggerated bloody "smiles" points to its possible origin.

Two different traditions of violent white-faced men in outlandish costumes apparently contributed to the clowns-in-vans phenomenon: the Klan/night doctors and clowns, the comic performers (they are complicated figures in their own right, with antecedents that include pagan wild men and medieval demons). This combination of elements apparently acquired a degree of reality during the clown flap.

Grim Rippers

On May 23, 1981, while clowns-in-vans were panicking children in Kansas City, a twenty-eight-year-old woman was abducted from Elmhurst, Illinois, near Chicago, and killed. She was the first of more than a dozen women murdered by the "Chicago Rippers" or "Ripper Crew," a team of four young serial killers—Robin Gecht, the brothers Andrew and Thomas Kokoraleis, and Edward Spreitzer.

They drove around Chicago and neighboring cities in a red van, grabbing women off the street and subjecting them to rape, torture, and murder. The Rippers also amputated one or both of the victims' breasts and allegedly ate them during satanic rituals. They were finally arrested in November 1982—but why discuss the Ripper crimes here?

There are parallels between the Chicago murders and clowns-in-vans, including when they began, how they were committed, and diabolical elements, but what is less apparent are the killers' personal connections to clowns. Robin Gecht was a former employee of "Pogo" himself, John Wayne Gacy, whose 1979 confession implicated Gecht in several murders. Gacy also befriended Andrew Kokoraleis on death row at the Menard Correctional Center.[43] He called the younger man "Koko," which is a predictable reduction of the multisyllabic *Kokoraleis* but also the name of a famous cartoon character, "Koko the Clown" from Max Fleischer's *Out of the Inkwell* series (1918–1929), and "Koko the Killer Clown," a surly dwarf who performs at Coney Island. Edward Spreitzer neither knew Gacy nor had a clownish nickname, but he did have a "big red fuzzy bush" of hair, "which stood up in all directions and he had clown lips." One detective thought he looked like the children's show marionette Howdy Doody, while the other was "immediately reminded of Bozo the Clown."[44]

Associates, nicknames, and appearances do not make the Chicago Rippers a physical embodiment of clowns-in-vans, but their cannibalism calls attention to the fear of being eaten that is a fundamental part of the clowns' origins.

Black Blood

Some Atlantans apparently believed that scientists were turning the blood of black children into interferon, the way earlier generations thought that blacks were kidnapped, cut up, and used to manufacture castor oil. Though cadavers were regularly stolen for anatomy classes, both modern and traditional night doctor legends can be understood from another perspective; as cannibalism described in terms of medicine. "Butchering" then becomes "dissection" and instead of victims being eaten as meat, they are reduced to the more palatable and presentable form of drugs. These stories represent an unexpected result of the slave trade; the "persistence of African beliefs that whites are maneaters."[45]

For hundreds of years, European and later American merchants sailed along the west coast of Africa buying vast numbers of slaves for transportation across the Atlantic in the Middle Passage. The physical conditions were horrific, but in addition to heat, filth, disease, and overcrowding were psychological terrors for Africans who had never seen the ocean or a ship, and thought white sailors were evil spirits. Rumors had spread

> from Senegambia to Angola that the slavers, whose appetite for human cargo had become prodigious, were insatiable cannibals . . . The white man's cannibalism explained his hunger for slaves and hence the trade.[46]

An eighteenth-century Dutch handbook advised traders to "assure the slaves . . . that they should not be afraid; that white people were not cannibals . . . ," but sailors would threaten to devour the captives, who interpreted the forced feedings and endless lying in chains as preparation for slaughter.[47]

For African slaves, the Middle Passage meant being chained into an incomprehensible conveyance and carried away as food for supernatural white-faced cannibals in bizarre clothing. The clowns-in-vans appear to be a stylized history of this ordeal, just as the Pied Piper of Hamelin seems based on the Children's Crusade.

Clowns, however, do not just represent night doctors or slave traders but the white race in general, which, according to folklore, needs black blood to live. Their unnatural pallor suggests coldness and death, while red mouths and noses are the gore-smeared faces of predators feeding on black victims—a belief born in Africa.

For example, consider a legend from Tanzania that was "apparently quite popular during World War II":

> A victim [African] would be rendered unconscious and then hung head down in order to let the blood from the

slit jugular drain into a bucket. The fluid was then transported by a fire engine to an urban hospital, where it was converted into red capsules. These pills were taken on a regular basis by Europeans who . . . needed these potations to stay alive in Africa.[48]

Phantom Clowns

Americans have been experiencing phantom panics since at least 1692, when spectral raiders menaced outlying farms at the outskirts of Gloucester, Massachusetts. Since then, there have been mysterious stabbers, snipers, gassers, wild men, and "Springheeled Jacks" (tall, thin figures that make superhuman leaps). Some of these have been reported for hundreds of years, but clowns-in-vans are a recent phenomenon, the result of a hypothetical union between black folklore and traditional clowns. The result was a modern form of phantom that spread rapidly, adapted to local conditions, and produced a number of different forms (e.g., the Chelsea Smilers).

Outbreaks of clown hysteria also provided an unusual complement to what was happening in popular culture, where the dark side of clowns, the "there's nothing funny about a clown in the moonlight" aspect, has assumed so much importance that the "evil clown" is one of the representative figures of contemporary horror.

Phantom clown panics still occur, but not on a nationwide scale. If they prove to be as durable as Springheeled Jack, and this theory of their origin is accurate, then Americans for generations to come will be haunted by grotesque, grease-painted, cannibal ghosts of the Middle Passage.

The Blood Gospel

The rumors circulating in Kansas City, Missouri, about a strange sect operating at the eastern part of the city had been dismissed as too fantastic to be true. At the beginning of 1890, William O. Huckett, secretary of the Humane Society, received a letter, however, that suggested it was time to investigate.

> Mr. Huckett: There is somethin I think ought to be called to your attenshun at once which I think is bad for a civilized community. their is John Wrinkle and his 2 children He has been sick and he is crazy on religion. his little Minnie is 13 years old and his boy John is 11. Wrinkle has hearn that people drink blod at the sloughter houses for their health an he said he believed in the bible that preached that the well should make sacrifises for the sick.

> He did blead his little boy and girl until they are recks and he did drink the blod. It has leaked out an unless something is done by you the neighbors will take the matter in their own hand and that quick too. He lives in a little piece of land near the new city limits. yours respectfully GEORGE WEST[1]

Secretary Huckett informed the chief of police, Thomas Speers, and a Humane Society officer named Marran was dispatched to the home of John Wrinkle, where he found

> two emaciated children. On the bed lay Wrinkle, who was apparently in the last stages of consumption. When questioned about drinking the blood of the children he strenuously denied having done so. The children also denied it. Their bloodless appearance, however, excited the suspicion of the officer and he compelled them to show their arms. The limbs were in a terrible condition, being covered with scars inside of the elbow joint, showing plainly the effects of the bleeding. When confronted with the evidence of the truth of the accusation, Wrinkle acknowledged that he had availed himself of the opportunity, and asserted that the children had willingly given their blood to restore him to health.[2]

No crime had been committed, but Minnie and John were placed in the Children's Home, while the moribund Wrinkle could not be moved. The blood drinking that appalled Mr. Wrinkle's neighbors would not end with his approaching death, though, for he was just one of Silas Wilcox's followers.

The Samaritans

Nothing is known about Silas Wilcox before his arrival in Kansas City in 1888 or 1889, but he was a traveling preacher who put great emphasis on helping the sick and interpreted Leviticus 17:11 (KJV), "For the life of the flesh is in the blood," to mean that blood cures disease. His teachings attracted around twenty believers who were called "the Samaritans" and visited slaughterhouses to drink "the blood of the freshly killed beeves."[3] At some point, however, Wilcox decided that it would be better if, instead of livestock, they drank each other's blood.

Perhaps it grew out of his conviction that the healthy must help the sick. Any reluctance the Samaritans might have felt about the new doctrine, however, was overcome by a dramatic demonstration of its power.

> Wilcox apparently became very sick and was unable to make the pilgrimage to the packing house. He called upon the faithful members of the band to volunteer to save his life. A woman named Nancy Dixon was the first to show her belief in the doctrine and she bared her arm

> for the extraction of the life-giving fluid. Wilcox sucked the blood from her arm and the effect was marvelous, for he recovered from his illness the same day. The visible manifestation of the truth of the doctrine made a great impression on the members of the band . . .[4]

After that they apparently stopped visiting slaughterhouses and assembled at a member's house each week and exchange blood. During these meetings, "the sick or ailing members ask for assistance from the well ones, and these are detailed to give their blood according to their health and strength. When a member becomes very sick the well ones take turns in supplying him the life-giving fluid."[5] Chief Speers was anxious to end the practice, but there was "no law which covers the case and nothing to be done."[6] The Samaritans also argued that "they have as much right to do this when the blood is a voluntary contribution as the physicians have to transfuse blood from one person to another."

Silas Wilcox and his disciples might have scandalized Kansas City residents and inspired headline writers to label them a "Hideous Sect" of "Human Vampires" and "A Band of Fanatics" engaged in "Horrible Practices," but hyperbole aside, a lot of blood drinking was going on at the time.[7]

Sanguinary Proceedings

In 1898, Joseph Ferdinand Gueldry's (1858–1945) painting *Buveurs de Sang* (*The Blood Drinkers*) caused a sensation at Paris's Salon des Artistes Français. Gueldry often depicted workshops and factories, but this slaughterhouse interior shocked many viewers. A description of the canvas appears in the July 24, 1898, *Brooklyn (NY) Daily Eagle*:

> The scene is a slaughterhouse. A powerful bull lies on the ground and the hammer that killed him is seen near the head. Blood has trickled and spattered over the vicinity. Whole beeves and sides and quarters hang on hooks about the large bare room. On the other side of the fallen animal are eight people, aged or sickly, who have assembled to drink the warm blood that pours from a rent in the animal's throat. One butcher is hauling at a cord and another stoops over the wound and hands the red fluid to the patients. A woman on whom a father is urging a glass of the disgusting medicine—or food, however it may be regarded—turns away and presses it back, unable to look at it.

The painting, which the *New York Times* described as "revoltingly disgusting," showed something that was apparently going on across the United States.[8] In addition to Kansas

City's packinghouses, blood drinking was reported in Albany; New York City; Cincinnati; St. Louis; New Orleans; and Johnstown, Pennsylvania.

Unlike French abattoirs, however, which retained elements of traditional butchering, American slaughterhouses were factories for killing animals and efficiently converting their bodies into meat, skin, and other marketable commodities (Henry Ford reportedly studied their *disassembly* methods and applied them to building cars). But even with this emphasis on speed, and the wine and sugar industry's demand for animal blood, an unknown number of slaughterhouses made themselves freely available for blood drinking; a St. Louis butcher said, "We do not charge for it so that the very poorest can take it if they desire."[9]

Blood drinkers—men, women, and children, of every age and class—arrived at the abattoir at times when animals were to be killed. Cattle from the stockyard were herded inside and driven single file down a chute to the killing floor, where a worker struck them on the head with a heavy sledgehammer. A stunned animal's throat was then cut and "as the current of life floods from the gash the cups and vessels are held to receive it, and it drank [*sic*] instantly with all the warmth of healthy vital action upon it."[10]

Neophytes had to become accustomed to the slaughterhouse atmosphere and swallowing hot blood, it seems to have been both palatable and digestible. Considered purely as a beverage, it was typically compared to drinking fresh milk and some developed a passion for it; one woman visited a New York City slaughterhouse every other day and downed "three full bumpers" of blood.[11] A Cincinnati reporter tried a tumbler of bullock's blood and became effusive, describing it as "the richest cream, warm, with a tart sweetness and the healthy strength of the pure wine that gladdeneth the hearts of man!"[12]

After draining their portion, the blood drinker might remain in the slaughterhouse for several hours "to inhale the 'steam' of the running blood."[13] Blood was also used externally; doctors ordered an Italian dancer to "bake her dainty ankle in bullock's blood," but most drank it and even developed their own set of standards.[14]

Some aficionados considered the blood of stunned animals to be "black and thick and lifeless" and preferred those dispatched by Jewish ritual slaughter, in which the throat is cut, claiming the results were "brightly ruddy and clear as new wine."[15] The source of the blood was also important, since there was far more to vital fluid than corpuscles and plasma.

One of the most ancient ideas about blood is that it is life and soul in material form, and its power can be transferred from one being to another, along with elements of the personality. This led to practices like drinking an enemy's blood to acquire his strength and bravery and applied to other important bodily fluids as well ("When it came to . . . the feeding of babies, actual nutrition was not the only thing taken in through female milk . . . it was the belief that *character was transmitted* through breast milk").[16] These considerations presumably influenced the blood drinkers' choice of animals.

Fowl, swine, sheep, and goats do not seem to have been used. Perhaps their blood was, respectively, too stupid, timid, slovenly, and lascivious; goat blood, in particular, was so potent that jewelers smeared it on precious stones to "soften" them before cutting. Though the ancient Greeks considered bulls' blood a deadly poison, cattle with their robust strength were seen as the ideal source of blood; they may have also appealed to the sometimes bovine standards of late-nineteenth-century beauty.

Woman who were pale, thin, and listless, or those emaciated by consumption were reportedly transformed by blood drinking. They became "wonderfully healthy and fat" or were turned into a "radiant beauty," though in the latter case this was accompanied by an insatiable craving for human blood.[17] (Modern "vampires" also believe that blood can enhance their appearance. Julia Caples of Wilkes-Barre, Pennsylvania, claims to drink as much as a half gallon of human blood a month and states that "I feel more beautiful than any other time when I'm regularly drinking").[18]

Blood was used to treat a range of ailments, including rheumatism, protracted fever, "impoverished blood," and extreme old age, but its most important use was for "[t]uberculosis, sometimes called consumption or pthisis, [which] was the greatest killer of 19th century Americans."[19] Wrinkle seems to have been afflicted with it, as were countless others, and for those who believed in its curative powers, treating the deadliest illness with human blood must have seemed logical.

Tapping the Vein

For thousands of years, the blood of children, virgins, and, oddly, executed criminals have been the most potent remedies in the pharmacopeia. A generally incurable disease (e.g., leprosy, blindness, or, for nineteenth-century Americans, consumption) "could only be removed by a miracle . . . the pure blood of a virgin or of a child was, above all, thought to be the source of life which would abolish those diseases and engender a flourishing new life . . ."[20]

The Egyptians, Babylonians, Greeks, and Romans used blood to treat epilepsy, and Pliny the Elder provides a vivid description of how it was taken. "While the crowd looks on," he writes, "epileptics drink the blood of gladiators, a thing horrible to see, even when wild beasts do it in the arena. Yet, by Hercules, they think it most efficacious to suck it as it foams warm from the man himself, and together with it the very soul out of the mouths of the wounds; yet it is not even human to put the mouth to the wounds of wild beasts."[21] It was a durable belief. In 1823, Hans Christian Andersen witnessed an execution at which "I saw a poor sick man, whom his superstitious parents made drink a cup of the blood of an executed person, that he might be healed of epilepsy . . ."[22]

Leprosy was especially dangerous for the subjects of kings who contracted it, since the recommended treatment was bathing in human blood. "The king of Egypt was eaten away. So he bade kill the first-born of the children of Israel, in order to bathe himself in their blood."[23] When Constantine the Great had leprosy, he was prepared to bathe in children's blood, but "the lamenting of the mothers moved the Emperor," who was miraculously cured after being baptized. It was also seen as a way to reinvigorate decrepit monarchs.[24]

Louis XI, like many other kings, was suspected of bathing in blood and, when very ill, "he seeks for and tries everything, especially much children's blood because of his illness."[25] The connection between blood baths and rejuvenation, however, reached its definitive form in the legend of Elizabeth Bathory, the "Blood Countess" of sixteenth-century Hungary.

Popular accounts claim that Bathory was extraordinarily beautiful and, as she grew older, tried preserving her appearance by murdering servant girls and bathing in their blood. There is no evidence that the countess engaged in these practices, and she was not accused of them at the time, but she was a serial killer who tortured and murdered as many as 650 girls over thirty years; perhaps folktales about restorative blood baths became attached to her as a way of comprehending the behavior of a sexual sadist. There is, however, no doubt that Bathory existed; the same cannot be said of Wilcox, the Wrinkles, or, the Samaritans.

Blood Test

Research has confirmed the existence of all the people mentioned in the story that held official positions. The Humane Society officer, T. Paul Marran, lived at 2203 Olive Street with his wife, who ran a bakery; William O. Huckett was secretary of the Kansas City Humane Society in 1890, and later became secretary of the police, while Thomas Speers was the town marshal when Kansas City was still on the frontier and served as chief of police from 1874 to 1895. Even the Children's Home that took in the young Wrinkles was at 1115 Charlotte Street. It later became known as the Gillis Home and still operates at a different location as the Gillis Center.

The story's principal figures, however, remain elusive.

No one named John Wrinkle, or anything comparable (e.g., "Winkle") appears in municipal or state records. There is no proof that he died in 1890, though deaths were not systematically recorded in Missouri before 1910, nor are there documents to show that Minnie and John went to the Children's Home; the Gillis Center's files do not go back to 1890. Silas Wilcox was an itinerant preacher and might be expected to leave little evidence behind, but there is another difficulty.

Newspaper articles about the Samaritans appeared in Wyoming, New York, and West Virginia but not Missouri. There are no follow-up reports, and the local historical society is unable to verify any aspect of it; "such a sensational treatment would surely have been covered in the *Kansas City Star* newspaper, though no story has yet been located."[26]

If the Kansas City blood cult is a hoax, it is a subtle one for 1890; that same year the *Tombstone (AZ) Epitaph* published an article about cowboys killing a giant winged reptile somewhere between Whetstone, Arizona, and the Huachuca Mountains. Though a penny-a-line journalist might have invented the story, it calls attention to the seemingly widespread and forgotten practice of blood drinking.

There were doctors who thought it might have genuine value (as noted in Dr. Gaetano De Pascale's "On the Use of Blood as a Medicine," which appeared in the May 5, 1866 *British Medical Journal*), but like shooting a pterodactyl with a Winchester rifle, blood drinking represents the intersection of two eras. It was a result of the nineteenth-century's industrial-scale slaughterhouses existing when ancient beliefs still thrived about blood as something "potent, full of latent life, and capable of working on persons or things in contact with it."[27]

AFTERWORD

Idiot Joy

Assembling a book of strange-but-true stories is, in most respects, a pleasure for the writer. It is an excuse to dig through accordion files full of old clippings, spend days online, write to librarians and historical societies, and turn over the sofa cushions in search of material. One of the greatest rewards, however, is the way researching one story leads to the discovery of others, such as monster-hunting expedition that Teddy Roosevelt considered making to Patagonia.

An American explorer and prospector reported seeing "a huge lizard-like monster with a curved neck" swimming in a South American lake, and the former president was so intrigued that he took a "special trip of exploration to Southern Argentina and Chile in the hope of ascertaining whether there was any truth in these stories of this monster amphibian, which strongly appealed to him. He wanted nothing said about it, lest there would be ridicule if he did not succeed."[1]

Then there was a Springheeled Jack–type figure nicknamed "Dracula" that terrorized residents of Baldwin, Long Island, in the summer of 1906. He was seen in trees, and police found several rude "nests" where he apparently slept. A witness described Dracula as tall, wild-eyed, and dressed in threadbare black clothing; his "hair was intensely black and he also wore a black mustache . . . his feet were incased [*sic*] in patent leather shoes, seemed small and that he apparently had little or no toes."[2] One hundred two years later, in 2008, a thin figure wearing a black cape and hood was spotted in a tree at Bethpage, and sightings of the "Long Island Devil" continued into 2009.

Even more puzzling is the filthy man found in the Sawyers' family barn at Westbrook, Maine, in 1854. He was around twenty-five years old and had been surviving by eating soap grease, drinking the cow's milk, and sleeping in a hole in the hay. Both of his feet had been crudely amputated, and he could only get about by crawling slowly on his knees, so how he even reached the Sawyers' farm is a mystery. The man was taken to the poorhouse and lived there at least twelve years, spending summers "in a sort of wooden cage-like structure in the yard."[3] He never spoke, so his identity, where he came from, and what happened to his feet, remains unknown.

A Swedish farmer named Burson also moved about on his

knees but claimed that he did so at God's command. The visionary Burson lived and preached at the Burned-Over District of western New York State, where he reportedly persuaded two hundred people to follow his example. Called the "Knee Benders," they went about on their knees, or all fours.[4]

Searching for more information about homemade beheading devices led to the story of George C. Wheeler, a young man who, in 1877, discovered a chemical for resurrecting the dead, no matter what the body's condition. He left instructions on how to apply the reviving agent, then climbed into a machine built from springs, knives, and an ax, and was torn to bits. Wheeler was real, but the report was a hoax, and he died of consumption in 1884.[5]

One story being saved for the next volume concerns the murder of an occultist and his family in Detroit, Michigan, in 1929. It is a fascinating case studded with strange elements that was not included here because the man's head was chopped off. Between the Sperry-Umberfield murders, James Moon's suicide, and various other decapitations, *Mrs. Wakeman vs. the Antichrist* was in danger of becoming *A Treasury of American Beheadings*. There is much more to discuss, yet the subject of future books suggests closing on a personal note.

After years of researching and writing something like *Mrs. Wakeman*, the sensible author takes a sabbatical from lunatics, monsters, and blood cults. There are people, however, with a seemingly magnetic attraction to whatever is eccentric and anomalous. As someone once told me, "I don't care who my parents are; I'm a member of the Addams family."

I am not the spokesman for those who consider every day Halloween, but I do know that what others consider bizarre often fills me with wonder and a kind of idiotic joy. That is why I began working on new stories before this book was even finished: Fortunately there is no dearth of strangeness in America.

—Robert Damon Schneck
May 2014

NOTES

The Wee-Jee Fiends

1 Most of the names and ages that appear here are taken from the 1920 census, where Italian names are often Anglicized. Reporters spelled the names in various ways (Nagarro Moro's name appears as both *Edward* and *Daniel)* and gave different ages.

2 Nagarro reportedly died in 1919. A different version of the story claims that Mrs. Moro wanted to remarry and that the group was trying to placate his spirit (*Oakland (CA) Tribune*, March 4, 1920).

3 One concerned group was Gypsies, who claimed that its fortune-telling businesses suffered from competition with the Ouija board (*Oakland Tribune*, September 24, 1920).

4 *Oakland Tribune*, February 1, 1920. The article mentions that five days earlier, a Ouija board had told two seventeen-year-old girls, Elsie Gerald and Florence Fuller, where a treasure could be found. The girls went looking for it in the frozen woods around Elk Rapids, Michigan, and were believed dead (*Capital Times (WI)*, January 28, 1920).

5 *Richmond (CA) News*, March 5, 1920. Folklorist Ruth Ann Musick collected a *dybbuk*-like story that reportedly happened at West Virginia in 1914 (*dybbuk* refers to a Jewish folk belief in posses-

sion by spirits of the dead, rather than demons). It involved Fred Brown, a coal miner, who became possessed by Sam Vincci, a miner who died two years earlier. Musick writes, "I have several other stories of possession, *all of Italian origin*, I believe [my italics]." Ruth Ann Musick, *The Bloody Lilac Bush* (Lexington, KY: University Press of Kentucky, 1965), 179.

6 *Oakland Tribune* (March 6, 1920). There were few black people in El Cerrito in 1920, but the name suggests a real person and not the generic "negro 'voodoo'" suggested by the *Richmond (CA) Independent* (March 5, 1920).

7 Different dates and times were reported for the Passion Display and learning the secret of the hole. The mystery of the hole was going to be revealed on March 7. According to the *Richmond Independent* (March 4, 1920), Rosa Bottini and her father believed that "[t]he 'evil spirits' were supposed . . . to disappear through a hole in the back yard at the Moro and Soldavini home, and the good spirits emerged from this hole."

8 The *Oakland Tribune* reported that the group burned any bill with a seven in its serial numbers. Other newspapers claimed that as much as $700 was destroyed, but Rosa Bottini said that only "small change" went into the fire (*Richmond Independent*, March 4, 1920). Newspaper accounts claimed that there were several Ouija boards in the house, but Rosa said: "It is queer that people should say there four. One is enough to give the messages" (*Oakland Tribune*, March 4, 1920). If the board was incinerated on March 1 or 2, it might reveal something about how the group was evolving with four psychics in one séance room: Mrs. Moro was "chief invoker of the power of the Ouija board"; Josephine had psychic dreams; Mrs. Bottini was a trance visionary; and Adeline, the spirit medium. Perhaps they had become competitive. If so, did the board's destruction represent Adeline's emergence as the leader? She was often described as their "high priestess."

9 Rosa is the only child who was identified. The Bottinis' three-year-old girl is mentioned in newspaper articles but not the census and

was probably there, along with the Soldavinis' children: two-year-old Eleanor and four-year-old "Masimo." (His name is difficult to read in the 1920 and 1930 censuses.) As for the fifth child, the *Oakland Tribune* reported that "the door of the shuttered house opened long enough for one of the group to dart out and seize a small child who was kept captive until the police arrived an hour later to find her brown curls had been added to the offerings." While this sounds improbable, the two-year-old son of Louis Francesco was reportedly missing for a brief period that day and was presumably the child found in the Moro-Soldavini house.

10 The idea that grimoires, books of spells, could not be destroyed or discarded has become part of Ouija board lore. This example comes from an online forum: "he took the board outside to the fire pit and lit it a fire, through [sic] the board into it, and the board came flying back at him, he tried that several times and each time it flew back at him. The last time, it hit his head and caused him to bleed (he still has the scar some 20 yrs later). Gave up on the fire and threw it in the trash. the next day she woke up and it was sitting on the bed stand by her bed." http://www.shadowsinthedarkradio.com/community.

11 *Lima (OH) Sunday News*, March 7, 1920.

12 *Richmond Independent*, March 6, 1920.

13 *Moberly (MO) Monitor-Index*, March 9, 1920. They were searching for the person who killed John Jones, an "old Welch hermit," nine years earlier, or perhaps Jones's missing treasure.

14 *Oxnard (CA) Daily Courier*, March 5, 1920.

15 *Lima Sunday News*, March 7, 1920. Rosicrucians claimed that "the Ouija board has nothing to do with spiritualism, or the claims of spiritualism, or even with the fundamental principles involved in real communication between disembodied personalities and earthly personalities."

16 William Brady, M.D., "Health Talks," *Appleton (WI) Post-Crescent*, October 12, 1920. The delusions were also seen as "readily communicable" (*Oakland Tribune*, March 5, 1920).

17 *Oakland Tribune*, August 1, 1920. Oakland had an outbreak of Ouija mania in 1919 involving three women: "One fully clothed, was walking calmly into a lake when rescued with difficulty. Another constantly 'heard mysterious voices.' The brilliant mind of the third had become shattered." *Charleston (WV) Daily Mail*, December 5, 1919.

18 http://www.bloodydisgusting.com/news/5290.

19 *Oakland Tribune*, March 4, 1920.

Mrs. Wakeman vs. the Antichrist

1 "Plenty of False Christs," *New York Times*, November 30, 1890.

2 "William Dorril: Early Religious Leader," *Greenfield (VT) Recorder*, June 12, 1984.

3 William Barton, "On the Manufacture and Marketing of a Religion," *The Independent*, January–December, New York, 1903.

4 *The Index: A Weekly Paper Devoted to Free Religion*, vol. 7 (1876), 438.

5 "Jones Cult Stirs Memory of Cobbites," *Arkansas Gazette*, December 28, 1978.

6 Ibid.

7 Andrew Jackson Davis, *Memoranda of Persons, Places and Events: Embracing Authentic Facts, Visions, Impressions, Discoveries, in Magnetism, Clairvoyance, Spiritualism. Also Quotations from the Opposition* (Boston: White, 1868).

8 Acts 7:52 (King James Version).

9 2 Kings 2:23–24 (KJV).

10 Robert P. Wakeman, *Wakeman Genealogy, 1630–1899* (Meriden, CT: Journal, 1900).

11 *New York Daily Tribune*, April 18, 1856.

12 *New York Daily Tribune*, January 31, 1856.

13 *New York Daily Tribune*, November 31, 1856.

14 *Skaneateles (NY) Democrat*, January 4, 1856, from the *Syracuse Chronicle*.

Notes

15 Similar lists appear in different newspapers, including the *Albany (NY) Evening Journal* (January 21, 1856), the *New York Daily Tribune* (January 21, 1856), and the *Auburn (NY) Daily American* (January 21, 1856).

16 *New York Times*, January 3, 1856.

17 *New York Times*, January 4, 1856.

18 Dr. E. C. Chamberlain testimony, Trial of the Wakemanites.

19 *Proceedings of the Worcester Society of Antiquity*, vol. 19 (1903).

20 *New York Times*, January 7, 1856.

21 Ibid.

22 *New York Daily Tribune*, January 21, 1856.

23 James Nelson testimony, Trial of the Wakemanites.

24 *New York Times*, January 7, 1856.

25 Ibid.

26 *New York Times*, December 28, 1855.

27 *New York Daily Tribune*, January 21, 1856.

28 Ibid.

29 Ibid.

30 "Trial of the Wakemanites," *New York Daily Tribune*, January 21, 1856.

31 *New York Times*, January 7, 1856.

32 Henry Wadsworth Longfellow, *The Poetical Works of Henry Wadsworth Longfellow*, vol. 3 (New York: Houghton Mifflin, 1902), 23.

33 *New York Times*, January 4, 1856.

34 Ibid.

35 *New York Times*, January 7, 1856.

36 *New York Daily Tribune*, January 21, 1856.

37 *New York Times*, May 10, 1879.

38 *New York Times*, January 7, 1856.

39 Ibid.

40 Ibid.

41 *New York Daily Tribune*, January 21, 1856.

42 Ibid.

43 Ibid.

44 Ibid.

45 *New York Times*, January 7, 1856.

46 *New York Daily Tribune*, January 21, 1856; *New York Times*, January 7, 1856.

47 *New York Times*, January 3, 1856.

48 *New York Times*, January 4, 1856.

49 Leviticus 17:11 (KJV).

50 *New York Times*, January 7, 1856.

51 Earl Wesley Fornell, *The Unhappy Medium* (Austin, TX: University of Texas Press, 1964).

52 "The Folk-Lore of British Plants," *The Dublin University Magazine*, vol. 82 (1873), 568.

53 *Scobie's Canadian Almanac and Repository of Useful Knowledge for the Year 1855* (Toronto: Hugh Scobie, n.d.).

54 "Woodbridge and the Wakemanites a Hundred Years Ago," paper read at the annual meeting of the Woodbridge and Amity Historical Society by Grace Pierpont Fuller, December 1955.

55 Ibid.

56 Israel Wooding testimony, Trial of the Wakemanites.

57 Almeron Sanford testimony, Trial of the Wakemanites.

58 Israel Wooding testimony, Trial of the Wakemanites.

59 *Wellespring* (newsletter of the Welles Family Association) (April 2004), 4.

60 *New York Times*, December 27, 1855.

61 *Weekly Hawkeye and Telegraph (IA)*, January 9, 1856.

62 *Wellespring* (April 2004).

63 Polly Sanford testimony, Trial of the Wakemanites.

64 Trial of the Wakemanites, quoted in "Woodbridge and the Wakemanites a Hundred Years Ago," paper read at the annual meeting of the Woodbridge and Amity Historical Society, by Grace Pierpont Fuller, December 1955.

65 "Woodbridge and the Wakemanites a Hundred Years Ago," paper read at the annual meeting of the Woodbridge and Amity Historical Society by Grace Pierpont Fuller, December 1955; J. W. Daniels, *Spiritualism versus Christianity* (1856).

66 *Delaware State Reporter*, January 1, 1856.

67 Donald MacLeod, *Life of Mary, Queen of Scots* (New York: Excelsior Catholic Publishing House, 1898). Dr. David L. Dagget performed the postmortem and found "a wound back of the ear, on the head, and another parallel with the lower jaw on the neck. There were two wounds penetrating the upper lip; the large wound commenced near the top of the spine and extended to the wind pipe. On the fore-finger of the left hand there was a wound. The wounds on the chest were evidently made with a fork. These wounds could not have been made by himself." Trial of the Wakemanites. This sort of violence, now called "overkill," indicates personal enmity, but Sammy denied having any ill will toward Matthews. Sly apparently expressed his anger toward Amos Hunt on the body of Justus Matthews.

68 Fornell, *The Unhappy Medium*, 97.

69 "Woodbridge and the Wakemanites a Hundred Years Ago," paper read at the annual meeting of the Woodbridge and Amity Historical Society by Grace Pierpont Fuller, December 1955.

70 *New York Times*, December 27, 1855.

71 Trial of the Wakemanites.

72 *New York Times*, December 27, 1855; *New York Times*, December 26, 1855.

73 *New York Daily Tribune*, February 5, 1856.

74 "Another Tragedy: Horrible Murders in Woodbridge," from a New Haven newspaper, January 3, 1856.

75 *New York Times*, January 4, 1856.

76 Ibid.

77 Ibid.

78 *Wellespring* (April 2004), quoting the *Hartford Daily Courant*, January 3, 1856, 1.

79 *New York Times*, January 4, 1856.

80 *The Journal of Psychological Medicine and Mental Pathology*, edited by Forbes Winslow, M.D., Vol. IX, London, John Churchill, New Burlington Street, MDCCCLVI, 1856. According to an appendix in Donald MacLeod's book, *Life of Mary, Queen of Scots*, Charles Sanford "stood over their corpses and gloated in the cry of 'blood, blood, how bright it seems and how easy it flows. Who would not have blood for the redemption of man?'"

81 *Reminiscences of Bethany.*

82 Ibid.

83 *New York Times*, January 4, 1856.

84 Samuel Davidson, "Seymour Record" (1913). Over time other versions of the story appeared. In one of them, Mrs. Wakeman declares that a man named Matthew is the devil, and "Charles Sanford, having become crazed with her teachings, had a brand new axe with which he planned to exterminate Matthews, with the idea that he would be doing a great service to the world and started on his way. First coming to a sleigh in which Enoch Sperry of Woodbridge was sitting on his way home from New Haven, Sanford came up behind the sleigh and deliberately chopped down his victim." *Reminiscences of Bethany.*

85 *New York Times*, January 3, 1856.

86 *New York Times*, January 4, 1856.

87 *West Virginia Archives and History News*, vol. 2, no. 1.

88 *New York Times*, January 4, 1856.

89 *New York Daily Times*, January 4, 1856.

90 The New Haven State House [date unknown], 17.

91 "Lies and Legends of Bethany," a talk given by Robert Brinton, OrangeBulletin.com.

92 Ibid.

93 Personal communication from Barbara Narendra to author, May 21, 2012.

94 *New York Times*, January 4, 1856. The online collection at http://www.findagrave.com does not list Enoch Sperry's grave at Westville, though it does have an "Enos Sperry," 1789–1873.

95 *New York Daily Tribune*, January 21, 1856.

96 *New York Daily Tribune*, January 31, 1856.

97 There is no reason for believing that Mrs. Wakeman was influenced by Freemasons, but the promise to have one's head taken off before leaving or forsaking the Savior recalls the Mason's oath to have his throat cut ear to ear if he betrays the group's secrets. In addition, there is Mrs. Wakeman's statement that her private papers "are only to be inspected by her few faithful followers who have taken *'all the degrees'*" [my italics]. *New York Daily Tribune*, January 31, 1856.

98 Fornell, *The Unhappy Medium*, 100.

99 *New York Times*, January 7, 1856.

100 Ibid.

101 Ibid.

102 *New York Times*, January 10, 1856.

103 *Daily Free Democrat (Milwaukee, WI)*, January 21, 1856.

104 *New Haven Courier* (January 18, 1856), printed in the *Tioga Eagle* (January 31, 1856).

105 "Trial of the Wakemanites," *New York Daily Tribune*, January 21, 1856.

106 *Daily Standard (Syracuse, NY)*, January 7, 1856.

107 Trial of the Wakemanites; *New York Times*, January 4, 1856.

108 *New York Daily Tribune*, January 21, 1856; Ephraim Lane testimony, Trial of the Wakemanites.

109 Phebe A. Beckwith testimony, Trial of the Wakemanites.

110 George Root testimony, Trial of the Wakemanites.

111 *New York Daily Tribune* [date unknown].
112 Trial of the Wakemanites.
113 Ibid.
114 Ibid.
115 *Fort Wayne (IN) Daily Times*, May 1, 1856.
116 Ibid.; Trial of the Wakemanites.
117 "Trial of the Wakemanites," *New York Daily Tribune*, January 21, 1856.
118 Ibid.
119 *Beckwith's Almanac*, no. 10 (1857).
120 Fornell, *The Unhappy Medium*, 101.
121 Herbert Hiram, *Poor Mary Stannard!* (New Haven, CT: Stafford, 1879), title page.
122 Ibid., 46.
123 *The Manson Women: An American Nightmare*, History Channel (2002).
124 Freeman was a leading member of the small Adventist community at Pocasset and, like the Wakemanites, was found not guilty by reason of insanity and committed to an asylum. He eventually recovered and was released.
125 *New York Times*, October 3, 1886.
126 *Encyclopedia Americana*, vol. 23 (1952), 218.

The Littlest Stigmatic

1 Oakland's Santa Fe Elementary School is at 915 54th Street, Oakland, California.
2 There is a surprising amount of confusion regarding her surname. It often appears as *Robinson*, sometimes as *Starks* and even *Cloretta Starks Robertson*. As she grew older, she used the name *Cloretta Starks*; presumably *Starks* is her biological father's name. When *Jet* magazine ran an article about her, however, they used *Robertson*

and it appears that way in newspaper ads placed by the family's church.

3 Loretta F. Early and Joseph E. Lifschutz, "A Case of Stigmata," *Archives of General Psychiatry* 30 (February 1974), 199. Another source claims that Cloretta read a book titled *Before the Cross.*

4 *Jet*, vol. 42, no. 3 (April 13, 1972), 14–15.

5 *The Times (San Mateo, CA)*, March 23, 1972.

6 Rene Biot, *The Enigma of the Stigmata* (Portland, OR: Hawthorn Books, 1962), 72.

7 St. Bonaventura, *Life of Saint Francis* (London: Dent, 1904), 137.

8 Ibid., 140.

9 Stanley Krippner, "Stigmatic Phenomena: An Alleged Case in Brazil," *Journal of Scientific Exploration* 16, no. 2 (2002), 207–224, 207.

10 Malcolm Day, "Blood Brother: Padre Pio," *Fortean Times* (September 2002).

11 Marco Margnelli, "An Unusual Case of Stigmatization," *Journal of Scientific Exploration* 13, no. 3 (1999), 463.

12 *The Times (San Mateo, CA)*, March 23, 1972.

13 *Arizona Republic*, March 24, 1972.

14 *The Times (San Mateo, CA)*, March 23, 1972.

15 Loretta F. Early and Joseph E. Lifschutz, "A Case of Stigmata," *Archives of General Psychiatry* 30 (February 1974), 197; *Daily Review (Hayward, CA)*, March 23, 1972.

16 *The Times (San Mateo, CA)*, April 1, 1972.

17 *New Castle (PA) News*, April 1, 1972.

18 *Daily Review (Hayward, CA)*, March 23, 1972.

19 *Jet*, vol. 42, no. 3 (April 13, 1972), 14–15.

20 Ibid.

21 *Daily Review (Hayward, CA)*, March 23, 1972.

22 *Stars and Stripes*, March 25, 1972.

23 *Daily Review (Hayward, CA)*, March 23, 1972.

24 Early and Lifschutz, "A Case of Stigmata," 197–200.

25 Ibid.

26 Ibid., 200.

27 Ibid., 197–200.

28 Stanley Krippner, "Stigmatic Phenomena: An Alleged Case in Brazil," *Journal of Scientific Exploration* 16, no. 2 (2002), 207–224.

29 Early and Lifschutz, "A Case of Stigmata," 199.

30 *Arizona Republic*, March 24, 1972.

31 Early and Lifschutz, "A Case of Stigmata," 199.

32 Ibid.

33 Ibid.; *Daily Review (Hayward, CA)*, March 23, 1972.

34 Early and Lifschutz, "A Case of Stigmata," 199.

35 Ibid.

36 *Oakland (CA) Tribune*, March 18, 1975.

37 The blood that appeared on the third day contained "hemoglobin, 12.9 gm/100 ml: white blood cells (WBC), 7,200; polymorphonuclear neutrophils, 70%: lymphocytes, 37%: monocytes, 3%; platelets, 246,000/cu mm; sickle cell preparation, negative results," Early and Lifshutz, "A Case of Stigmata," 199.

38 Ibid., 199–200.

39 *Mountain Democrat (Placerville, CA)*, July 5, 1973.

40 Early and Lifschutz, "A Case of Stigmata," 198.

41 Ibid., 200.

42 Ibid., 199.

43 Ibid.

44 Ibid., 200.

45 *Jet*, vol. 42, no. 3 (April 13, 1972), 14–15; *Daily Review (Hayward, CA)*, April 1, 1972.

46 Early and Lifschutz, "A Case of Stigmata," 200.

47 *Oakland Tribune*, March 18, 1975.

48 *Oakland Tribune*, April 4, 1975.

49 Early and Lifschutz, "A Case of Stigmata," 200.

50 *Oakland Tribune*, October 7, 1977.

51 Claudia Mair Burney, *Wounded: A Love Story* (Colorado Springs, CO: Cook, 2008), 133–134.

52 "Holy Enigma," *People*, April 27, 1992.

The Four Wild Men of Dr. Dedge

1 An *Almas* is a Central Asian wild man; the city might be named after Mrs. Alma Sheridan, or the combined initials of the four cities that have been Georgia's capital: Augusta, Louisville, Milledgeville, and Atlanta.

2 Personal communication from Judge Braswell Deen to author, November 16, 2009.

3 Ivan Sanderson, *Things* (New York: Pyramid Books, 1967), 80–93.

4 *New York Times*, February 10, 1883; *New York Times*, August 19, 1884.

5 *Atlanta Constitution*, February 4, 1889.

6 Robert Bogdan, *Freak Show* (Chicago: University of Chicago Press, 1990), 60.

7 Ibid.

8 "The Wild Men of Borneo! or Modern Sampsons, Recently the Great Sensation in Boston, and Eastern Cities. The Greatest Curiosities Ever Seen By Man." http://www.barnummuseumexhibitions.org/apps/blog/entries/show/17850627-wild-men-of-borneo.

9 Ibid.

10 "What is It?" or "Man Monkey." Lithograph (circus poster) by Currier & Ives, c. 1860. Negative #67612. From the collection of the New-York Historical Society; Frederick Drimmer, *Very Special People* (New York: Bantam, 1973).

11 Charles Carroll, *The Negro a Beast* (St. Louis, MO: American Book and Bible House, 1900), 148.

12 Ibid., title page.

13 Alexander Winchell, *PreAdamites* (Chicago: Griggs, 1881), 178.

14 *Milledgeville (GA) Statesman*, June 6, 1829.

15 The Baxley (GA) News Banner, June 9, 1938, George D. Lowe, "Rambling Remarks and Reminiscences."

16 Dr. Dedge vaccinated seven hundred employees of the Southern Pine Company at Waycross on January 26, 1900. *Atlanta Constitution*, February 1, 1900.

17 *Des Moines News*, June 26, 1914. Information about Doc Brinson's sideshow career comes from an unsourced article at the Alma Historical Society. According to the *Des Moines News* (June 26, 1914), Brinson was a successful businessman who "turned down innumerable offers from circus and vaudeville people, preferring his happy life on the farm."

18 Scott Hart, "How Circus Freaks Are Made," *Coronet* (May 1946).

19 *Newark (OH) Daily Advocate*, March 15, 1883.

20 A copy exists of Dedge's passport application, dated July 5, 1901.

21 Lovick Pierce Anthony, *A Dictionary of Dental Science* (Philadelphia and New York: Lea and Febiger, 1922), 169.

22 *Atlanta Constitution*, July 20, 1904.

23 *The Post Standard (NY)*, August 21, 1902.

24 Lowe, "Rambling Remarks and Reminiscences."

25 Ibid.

26 *Atlanta Constitution*, July 20, 1904. The newspaper also reported that Dr. Dedge had secured the wild man in Central America, which agrees with Bird's account of where they met.

27 http://www.syracuse.ny.us/parks/kirkpark.html.

28 *The Post-Standard (NY)*, August 21, 1902.

29 *The Post-Standard (NY)*, August 22, 1902.

30 Ibid.

31 Ibid.

32 *The Post-Standard (NY)*, August 23, 1902.

33 Unsourced article from the Alma Historical Society, 62.

34 "Discussion on the Paper of Dr. Roberts," *The Illinois Medical Journal*, February 1911, 19: 221.

Notes

35 *Atlanta Constitution*, July 20, 1904.

36 Victoria and Frank Logue, *Touring the Backroads of North and South Georgia* (Winston-Salem, NC: John F. Blair), 198; *Atlanta Constitution*, July 20, 1904.

37 Lowe, "Rambling Remarks and Reminiscences."

38 Unsourced article from the Alma Historical Society, 62.

39 *Atlanta Constitution*, July 20, 1904.

40 Lowe, "Rambling Remarks and Reminiscences."

41 *Atlanta Constitution*, February 20, 1910.

42 Ibid.

43 Ibid.

44 *Atlanta Constitution*, March 6, 1913.

45 Ibid.

46 Ibid.

47 Arthur D. Little and Arthur D. Little Jr., "The Goat Man," reprinted from *Medical Mentor* 4, no. 2 (April 1933), 132.

48 Ibid., 132–133.

49 Ibid., 133.

50 Ibid.

51 Ibid.

52 http://meddersfamilyresearch.org/Charles%20J%20Medders.htm.

53 Unsourced article from the Alma Historical Society, 62.

54 Ibid.

55 This source also reports that Brinson died on the same day as Dedge, August 16, 1926. http://www.time.com/time/magazine/article/0,9171,722337,00.html. Brinson's tombstone, however, says August 4. http://www.findagrave.com.

56 Personal communication from Judge Braswell Deen to author, November 18, 2009.

57 Patrick Gerster and Nicholas Cords, *Myth and Southern History: The Old South*, vol. 1 (Champaign: University of Illinois Press, 1989), 94.

58 Barbara Holden-Smith, "Lynching, Federalism and the Intersection of Race and Gender in the Progressive Era," *8 Yale Journal of Law and Feminism* 31 (1996), 16.

59 Ibid., 47.

60 J. C. Cooper, *An Illustrated Encyclopedia of Traditional Symbols* (London: Thames and Hudson, 1978), 84; Gail Bederman, *Manliness and Civilization* (Champaign: University of Chicago Press, 1995), 49.

61 Cooper, *An Illustrated Encyclopedia*, 144.

62 https://twitter.com/deen_jr.

63 http://www.evolutionornot.com/pages/wildmanofokefenokee.html. Judge Deen's writings are available for free download at his website (http://www.evolutionornot.com), along with audio commentaries.

Holy Geist

1 The land was originally in Frederick County, which became Berkeley County, Virginia. During the Civil War, West Virginia separated from Virginia and joined the Union in 1863. Livingston's land is now in Jefferson County, West Virginia.

2 Adam married twice. His first wife's name has been lost, but the second might have been named Mary Ann. There are references to the second Mrs. Livingston, as the children's stepmother, so the first wife presumably gave birth to all eight. They were Henry, Eve, George, Mary Ann, Charlotte, Agnes, Jacob, and Catherine. It is not known which wife went to Virginia. In addition, Adam's sister inherited a smaller adjacent property and moved there with her husband, and Adam seems to have owned four slaves. None of these people appear in accounts of the poltergeist.

3 The parents of Father Demetrius Augustine Gallitzin (1770–1840) were intimates of Voltaire. Gallitzin became a Roman Catholic at age seventeen, arrived in America in 1792, and became the first

priest to receive all his training and orders in the United States. He died in 1840, and in 2005 the Church declared Gallitzin a "Servant of God." The town of Gallitzin, Pennsylvania, was named in his honor and has several points of Fortean interest. See http://www.demetriusgallitzin.org.

4 Joseph Finotti, *The Mystery of the Wizard Clip* (Baltimore: Kelly, Piet, 1879), 85.

5 Ibid., 127.

6 Letter from Father Gallitzin to Mrs. Catherine C. Doll, April 11, 1839.

7 Finotti, *The Mystery of the Wizard Clip*, 21.

8 Demetrius A. Gallitzin, *Gallitzin's Letters* (Loretto, PA: 1940), 221–222; A. E. Marshall, *Adam Livingston: The Wizard Clip, The Voice* (Kearneysville, West Virginia: Livingston Publications, 1978), 16.

9 Gallitzin's Letters, 221–222; Marshall, *Adam Livingston*, 11.

10 The Irish peddler might have inspired the "Unknown Stranger" legend; both result in Livingston finding a priest. Finotti, *The Mystery of the Wizard Clip*, 91–92.

11 In Mrs. McSherry's account, Livingston had a dream about a robed man who would end Adam's suffering; when he recognized Father Cahill as the man in his dream, he wept "bitterly." Father Gallitzin states that Richard McSherry convinced a reluctant Livingston to have a priest at the house and then argued with Father Cahill until he agreed to go there.

12 Finotti, *The Mystery of the Wizard Clip*, 92.

13 Marshall, *Adam Livingston*, 27.

14 There is a single reference to young children being able to see the Voice but no description of its appearance.

15 A sixteenth-century French poltergeist (Lyon, 1525–1526) also confirmed the doctrine of Purgatory. "It has sometimes been hinted that the affair was got up to dish the Lutherans, whose views on purgatory it appeared to controvert." Alan Gauld and A. D. Cornell, *Poltergeists* (Boston: Routledge and Kegan Paul, 1979), 23. In

some respects, the Wizard-Voice seems like a religious version of Tennessee's Bell Witch.

16 Handprints burned into objects by souls in Purgatory can be seen at the Church of St. Romedius in Thaur, Austria, and the Museum of the Souls in Purgatory in the Sacro Cuore del Suffragio church in Rome, which has a collection of them.

17 The story of the Angel is similar to the Wandering Jew, encounters with the Mormon Nephites, and some vanishing hitchhikers.

18 Raphael Brown, *The Mystery of the Wizard Clip* (Wheeling, WV, Catholic Diocese of Wheeling-Charleston, 1990), 31.

19 Marshall, *Adam Livingston*, 31–34.

20 Parapsychologist Raymond Bayless claimed to have identified the agent, writing: "Apparitions were said to have commonly occurred and a girl who was obviously the unwitting, inadvertent medium, suffered so from unwelcome attentions of the poltergeist that she was believed near death at one time." Raymond Bayless, *The Enigma of the Poltergeist* (West Nyack, NY: Parker, 1967), 21. Bayless must have been working from a very different version of the story.

21 Marshall, *Adam Livingston*, 34.

22 In his pamphlet *The Legend of the Wizard Clip and . . . The Other Story* (C.O.P.E. International, 1983), James Dale Nordheim argues that the phenomena had been faked as part of a Jesuit conspiracy to acquire Livingston's land. He also claimed the Jesuits murdered Pope Clement XIV and that the crescents had occult significance.

23 Finotti, *The Mystery of the Wizard Clip*, 88.

24 Ibid., 70–71, 104.

The Man in Room 41 and Other Decapitants

1 *Rhinelander (WI) Daily News*, March 28, 1951.

2 *Salt Lake Tribune (UT)*, April 27, 1901.

Notes

3 "Characteristic Features of Deaths due to Decapitation," abstract, *American Journal of Forensic Medicine and Pathology* 26, no. 2 (2005), 198.

4 "Vehicle Assisted Decapitation: A Case Report," *American Journal of Forensic Medicine and Pathology* 33, no. 1 (2012), 73–75.

5 *Weimar Mercury (CO)*, June 14, 1935.

6 *Portsmouth (NH) Herald*, February 5, 1901. This item appeared in many newspapers, but the source is unknown.

7 *American Practitioner*, August 11, 1876.

8 Ibid.

9 *New York Times*, June 15, 1876.

10 *American Practitioner*, August 11, 1876.

11 *Washington (DC) Herald*, June 7, 1908; *Journal and Courier*, October 22, 1989.

12 *Sunday Morning Leader*, June 18, 1876.

13 *Lafayette City Directory*, http://bangingonthedrum.blogspot.com/2012/04/wonderful-suicide-bridget-clogan.html.

14 http://bangingonthedrum.blogspot.com/2011_11_01_archive.html.

15 *Boston Medical and Surgical Journal* 95 (June–December 1876).

16 *Journal and Courier*, Lafayette, Indiana November 5, 1989.

17 Dr. W. W. Vinnedge, "The Moon Suicide," *American Practitioner*, August 11, 1876; *Journal and Courier*, November 19, 1989.

18 *Journal and Courier*, October 29, 1989.

19 *Fort Wayne (IN) Sentinel*, June 28, 1876.

20 *Journal and Courier*, October 29, 1989.

21 *Sunday Morning Leader*, June 18, 1876.

22 "About the City," a collection of articles about Moon from the Lafayette Historical Society, June 18, 1876.

23 Dr. William Bennett and John Cribb, *The American Patriots Almanac* (Nashville: Nelson, 2008), 595.

24 *Sunday Morning Leader*, June 25, 1876; *Sunday Morning Leader*, June 18, 1876.

25 Leonard DeVries, *'Orrible Murder* (New York: Taplinger, 1971), 31.

26 *Sunday Morning Leader*, June 25, 1876.

27 Ibid.

28 *Journal and Courier*, November 12, 1989.

29 *Newark (OH) Daily Advocate*, April 8, 1901.

30 *New York Times*, April 18, 1894.

31 *Illustrated Police News*, May 22, 1880, featured in DeVries, *'Orrible Murder*, 146–147.

32 *Fitchburg (MA) Daily Sentinel*, July 21, 1880.

33 *Journal and Courier*, June 23, 1951.

34 *Journal and Courier*, October 29, 1989.

35 *New York Times*, February 12, 1876.

36 *American Practitioner*, August 1876.

37 *Elkhart (IN) Sentinel*, July 18, 1889.

Bigfoot's Gold: The Secret of Ape Canyon

1 Richard W. Wrangham, *Chimpanzee Cultures* (Boston: Harvard University Press, 1996), 85.

2 Cowlitz County Historical Society, *History of Cowlitz County, Washington* (Dallas, TX: Taylor, 1983).

3 http://en.wikipedia.org/wiki/Kelso,_Washington.

4 *Cowlitz County Historical Quarterly*, vol. 5, no. 1 (May 1963).

5 Cowlitz County Historical Society, 1957.0109.0003 Print, Photographic.

6 *Cowlitz County Historical Quarterly*, vol. 5, no. 1 (May 1963).

7 Fred Beck, *I Fought the Apeman* (self-published), 1967.

8 June Beck Perry and Virginia Beck Hanks (with help from Dorothy Beck Sturdivant), *Rambling Rose of Paw-Paw Grove* (1988), 133.

9 Ibid.

10 Lewis Spence, *Encyclopedia of Occultism and Parapsychology, Part 2* (Whitefish, MT: Kessinger, 2003).

11 William Benjamin Hayden, *On the Phenomena of Modern Spiritualism* (Boston: Otis Clapp, 1855), 130.

12 *American Spiritual Magazine*, vol. 2 (Boyle & Company, Memphis, 1876), 366.

13 *Eugene (OR) Register-Guard*, July 15, 1924.

14 Michael Perry, "The Story behind the Great Ape Hunt of 1924," *Columbia River Reader*, October 15–November 14, 2009. The author of the article is Fred Beck's grandnephew.

15 Beck, *I Fought the Apeman*.

16 Rene Dahinden or Larry Lund might have the rifle Beck used at Ape Canyon. I was unable to locate the current owner. Personal communication from Christopher L. Murphy to author, June 1, 2010.

17 Over the years, Beck told several different versions of the ax incident.

18 When interviewed by Roger Patterson, Beck provided more details, saying, "one of them fellas run out of a clump of bush and run down the gorge, and I shot him in the back, three shots, and I could hear the bullets hit him and see the fur fly on his back. I shot for his heart. And he stopped and just fell right over a precipice, and I heard him go doonk, zoop, down into the canyon . . . that water was really a torrent goes down there, it'd wash anything out fall in there." 1966 interview with Fred Beck about Bigfoot attack. http://trees.ancestry.com/tree/4552813/person/-1578396877/story/4b211d7b-cb3d-465e-8d96-5bf58388afa0?src=search.

19 Perry and Hanks, *Rambling Rose of Paw-Paw Grove*, 133.

20 Michael McLeod, *Anatomy of a Beast: Obsession and Myth on the Trail of Bigfoot* (Berkeley: University of California Press, 2009), 95.

21 *Manitoba Free Press (Winnipeg, Canada)*, July 16, 1924.

22 *Oakland (CA) Tribune*, July 17, 1924.

23 *Lebanon (OR) Daily News*, June 25, 1964.

24 Beck, *I Fought the Apeman*.

25 Ibid.

26 In 1951 a logger discovered Ape Cave, which was named after the local Boy Scout troop that explored it. They called themselves "the Apes," apparently because of their interest in the ape-men of local Indian folklore; that seems to be the cave's only connection to Bigfoot.

27 Perry and Hanks, *Rambling Rose of Paw-Paw Grove*, 132.

28 Personal communication from John D. Pickering to author, June 6, 2010.

29 Perry and Hanks, *Rambling Rose of Paw-Paw Grove*, 133.

30 Perry, "The Story behind the Great Ape Hunt of 1924."

31 Perry and Hanks, *Rambling Rose of Paw-Paw Grove*, 134.

32 Ibid., 133.

33 John Green, *On the Track of Sasquatch* (Surry, British Columbia, and Blaine, WA: Hancock House Publishers, Third Edition, 1994), 48.

34 Perry and Hanks, *Rambling Rose of Paw-Paw Grove*, 154–156.

35 Personal communication from John Green to author, May 27, 2010.

36 http://www.youtube.com/watch?v=Xxq8h-ymPr0.

37 Beck, *I Fought the Apeman*.

38 Personal communication from John D. Pickering to author, June 6, 2010; Jerome Clark, *Unexplained!* (Detroit, MI: Visible Ink Press, 1998), 335.

39 Personal communication from Michael Perry to author, December 11, 2009.

40 Personal communication from John Green to author, May 27, 2010.

41 *Longview Daily News (Longview, WA)*, June 27–28, 1964.

42 Personal communication from Christopher L. Murphy to author, May 31, 2010.

43 Personal communication from Christopher L. Murphy to author, June 1, 2010 [my italics].

44 Franklin C. Jillson and Mary Jillson, *Green Leaves from Whitingham, Vermont: A History of the Town* (private press, 1894), 116; Walter R. Hard and Janet C. Greene, "Mischief in the Mountains," *Vermont Life* (1970), 128.

45 Ruth Ann Musick, *The Bloody Lilac Bush*, 68–69.

46 D. Michael Quinn, *Early Mormonism and the Magic World View* (Salt Lake City, UT: Signature Books, 1998), 25.

47 Jillson and Jillson, *Green Leaves from Whitingham, Vermont*, 119.

48 Mark Ashurst-McGee, "Moroni as Angel and as Treasure Guardian," *FARMS Review*, vol. 18, no. 1 (2006), 34–100.

49 *Indiana Progress*, March 16, 1870; Colonial Society of Massachusetts, *Transactions 1917–1919*, vol. 20 (Published by the Society, Boston, 1920), 357.

50 Ashurst-McGee, "Moroni as Angel and as Treasure Guardian," 45.

51 *Law Notes* 12 (E. Thompson Company, January 1907), 191.

52 *Wait v. Westfall* (161 Ind. 648).

53 Grillot de Givry, *Witchcraft, Magic and Alchemy* (New York: Dover, 1971), 172–173.

54 Beck, *I Fought the Apeman*.

55 Ibid.

56 Ivan Sanderson, *Abominable Snowmen: Legend Come to Life* (New York: Chilton, 1974), 51.

57 Ibid., 53.

58 Beck, *I Fought the Apeman*.

59 Jack "Kewaunee" Lapseritis, *The Psychic Sasquatch and Their UFO Connection* (Mill Spring, NC: Wild Flower Press, 1998), 22.

60 Richard W. Kimball, "Bigfoot Lives in the Arizona Wilds," *Chino Valley Review*, December 12, 1990. http://members.tripod.com/Arizona_Bigfoot/bf1.htm.

61 Ibid.

62 *The (Frederick, MD) News*, July 30, 1892.

63 Linda Godfrey, *Hunting the American Werewolf* (Madison, WI: Trails Media Group, 2006), 255–256.

64 Ibid.

65 Mary Granger, *Drums and Shadows* (Athens, GA: University of Georgia Press, 1940).

66 *Longview Washington Times* (August 1963). http://www.bigfootencounters.com/articles/spiritlake.htm.

67 Hans Biedermann, *Dictionary of Symbols* (New York: Plume, 1994), 350.

Psychic in the White House

1 The Jeane Dixon Museum and Library was at 132 North Massanutten Street, Strasburg, Virginia, http://archive.today/p9vdm, originally http://www.waysideofva.com/jdml/default.htm.

2 Mike the MagiCat was the subject of a children's book, *Jeane Dixon's MagiCat*. Some saw Dixon's affinity for cats as that of a witch for her familiar. President Harry S. Truman had a cat with the same name.

3 She elaborates on the idea in *Yesterday, Today and Forever* (New York: Morrow, 1976). Aries is identified with Peter, Taurus with Simon, Gemini with James the Less, and so on. Pisces is both Judas Iscariot and Matthias.

4 "In Strasburg, a Medium Well Done," *Washington Post*, July 31, 2002. www.washingtonpost.com/wp-dyn/content/article/2002/07/31/AR2005033107245.html.

5 Ruth Montgomery, *A Gift of Prophecy* (New York: Bantam Books, 1966), 18.

6 Dixon was a "dollar-a-year man," a business executive who accepted a token salary for performing government service; he acquired warehouses and depots.

7 Much of the information in this section comes from Daniel St. Albin Greene, "The Untold Story of Jeane Dixon," *National Observer*, October 27, 1972.

8 Denis Brian, *Jeane Dixon: The Witnesses* (New York: Doubleday, 1976), 147–148. When Daniel St. Albin Greene was researching "The Untold Story of Jeane Dixon," he received telegrams from Dixon's siblings stating that she had been born in 1918. He spoke to Curt Pinckert before the article was published, yet Curt had no recollection of sending a telegram and confirmed that Jeane Dixon was born Lydia Pinckert in 1904.

9 Greene, "The Untold Story of Jeane Dixon." "In January 1928, according to a marriage certificate on file in Santa Ana, Calif., 'Jeane A Pinckert,' daughter of Frank and Emma Pinckert, married Charles Zuercher, a Swiss immigrant who had come to California the same year the Pinckerts did. The document says the groom was a 37-year-old 'superintendent,' the bride an accountant, aged '22.'"

10 Brian, *Jeane Dixon: The Witnesses*, 198.

11 Montgomery, *A Gift of Prophecy*, 33.

12 Ibid., 77. Four years later, Jeane claimed that James wanted her to devote herself to charitable and psychic pursuits, but she felt that working kept her grounded. Rene Noorbergen, *My Life and Prophecies* (New York: Morrow, 1969), 26–27.

13 Greene, "The Untold Story of Jeane Dixon."

14 Harvey Katz, "The Jeane Dixon Touch (II): This Is No Way to Run a Charity," *Washingtonian* (March 1970), 49.

15 "Another merry time was had by 288 top Congressmen and government officials who thronged a white tie dinner-dance tossed by former TV glamour-girl Martha Rountree and her publisher husband, Oliver Presbrey . . . 300 chickens, 150 lobsters and platters of flaming cherries jubilee vied for attention with two dance orchestras and fortune-telling Jeane Dixon until well past curfew." *Sunday Times (Cumberland, MD)*, February 12, 1956.

16 Montgomery, *A Gift of Prophecy*, front cover blurb.

17 Dixon saw the statue's face come to life in 1958 when the cathedral seemed filled with people of every race and religion in what she

claimed was a vision of Vatican II. Presumably, the sculpture she referred to once stood in the Lady chapel, which was smashed by a vandal in the early 1980s and replaced in 1984 by the unusual statue that now occupies the spot. Jeane Dixon had other visions in St. Matthew's, including a fully materialized Blessed Virgin Mary, two diabolical red boots that walked around a side altar, a vision of the zodiac that assigned astrological signs to particular apostles, and a wheel-shaped medical center.

18 Ibid.

19 Jack Anderson and Fred Blumenthal, "Washington's Incredible Crystal Gazer," *Parade*, May 13, 1956, 12.

20 Brian, *Jeane Dixon: The Witnesses*, 191.

21 Ibid., 60.

22 Ibid., 192; Montgomery, *A Gift of Prophecy*, 11.

23 Brian, *Jeane Dixon: The Witnesses*, 192.

24 Montgomery, *A Gift of Prophecy*, 192–193.

25 Mary Bringle, *Jeane Dixon: Prophet or Fraud?* (Gainesville, FL: Tower, 1970), 69.

26 Montgomery, *A Gift of Prophecy*, 174.

27 Ibid., 180.

28 Gordon Lindsay, *The Mystery of Jeane Dixon: Prophetess or Psychic Medium?* (Dallas, TX: Christ for the Nations Institute, 1973), 29.

29 "Miss Dixon: Door Open, But Can GOP Get In?" *Gastonia Gazette*, October 24, 1967.

30 Helen Thomas: "White House Calls Book Vengeful," *Tyrone (PA) Daily Herald*, May 10, 1988.

31 Dixon, *Yesterday, Today and Forever*, 424.

32 Montgomery, *A Gift of Prophecy*, 107.

33 Jeane Dixon, *Jeane Dixon's Astrological Cookbook* (New York: Morrow, 1976), 17. Montgomery was the first of several unhappy collaborators. She claimed that her editor and Dixon had pressured her into writing the book ("Mrs. Dixon . . . has been insisting that I

write a book about her since 1960"), that the editor had removed most of the wrong predictions, and that commercial success had interfered with Dixon's powers. Rene Noorbergen, of *My Life and Prophecies,* was "convinced Jeane is inspired by the devil." Brian, *Jeane Dixon: The Witnesses,* 145.

34 The model was displayed at the Jeane Dixon Museum. Circular layouts are often associated with visionaries, including Laputa, Atlantis, the City of the Sun, John Murray Spear's circular cities, and Walt Disney's plans for Epcot.

35 Katz, "The Jeane Dixon Touch (II)," 51.

36 "Dangers of Being a Nation of Number Numbskulls," *New York Times,* January 23, 1989.

37 Memorandum from unnamed special agent in the Washington field office to J. Edgar Hoover, January 28, 1966.

38 Memorandum from Mr. Wick to M. A. Jones, February 4, 1966.

39 Letter from Jeane L. Dixon to the Federal Bureau of Investigation, January 2, 1970.

40 Memorandum from Mr. DeLoach to T. E. Bishop, January 13, 1970.

41 Joe Beaird, "Psychic Jeane Dixon Was FBI Stooge," December 27, 1999. lists.village.virginia.edu/lists___archive/sixties-1/2335.html. Letter from correspondent (name removed) to J. Edgar Hoover, February 16, 1968.

42 Letter from correspondent (name removed) to Sen. Hale Boggs, April 1971.

43 According to American National Biography Online, Dixon was godmother to Senator Strom Thurmond's son and contributed at least $30,000 to the Republican Party in the last ten years of her life.

44 Thomas, "White House Calls Book Vengeful." Jeane Dixon was neither the first nor last psychic to become involved with presidents and their families. Mrs. Franklin Pierce met with Maggie Fox, Mary Todd Lincoln engaged several mediums, and her hus-

band attended at least one White House séance. More recently, Mrs. Clinton held "imaginary conversations" with the late Eleanor Roosevelt.

45 Michael Isikoff and Mark Hosenball, "Terror Watch: Nixon and Dixon," *Newsweek*, March 23, 2005. http://www.newsweek.com/id/48973.

46 Bringle, *Jeane Dixon: Prophet or Fraud?*, 136.

47 J. Edgar Hoover, quoted in an FBI memorandum from M. A. Jones to Mr. Wick, February 4, 1966. Denis Brian's book, *Jeane Dixon: The Witnesses*, might be the fairest evaluation of her record.

48 Jeane Dixon had long been associated with Billy Graham, especially by conspiracy-minded and lunatic writers. See "Billy Graham's Active Role in Satanic Ritual Abuse," www.whale.to/b/sp/for1.html, and "Will Teddy Listen to the Prophet?", *Cedar Rapids (IA) Gazette*, June 16, 1968.

49 Descriptions taken from the auction catalog *Sloans & Kenyon: Estate of Psychic Jeane Dixon*, Sloans & Kenyon, Chevy Chase, Maryland, July 26, 2009.

Ku Klux Klowns

1 Loren Coleman generously explained how he discovered, researched, and named the clowns-in-vans for this book. Personal communication from Loren Coleman to author, January 10, 2014.

2 Memo from Daniel O'Connor, investigative counselor of the Boston Public School District, to elementary and middle school principals. Quoted in Loren Coleman, *Mysterious America* (Boston: Faber and Faber, 1983), 266.

3 Joseph A. Citro, *Weird New York* (New York: Sterling Publishing, 2005), 32.

4 Associated Press, May 23, 1981.

Notes

5 United Press International, May 23, 1981.

6 United Press International, May 24, 1981.

7 Associated Press, May 23, 1981.

8 Ibid.

9 United Press International, May 24, 1981.

10 Milton Meltzer, *Slavery (I)* (Chicago: Cowles, 1971), 189.

11 Gladys-Marie Fry, *Night Riders in Black Folk History* (Chapel Hill: University of North Carolina Press, 1975), 87–88.

12 KKK Report, Georgia, 649, quoted in Fry, *Night Riders in Black Folk History*, 123.

13 Fry, *Night Riders in Black Folk History*, 115–116.

14 *Charleston (SC) Mercury*, October 12, 1838, 171, reprinted in Theodore D. Weld, *American Slavery as It Is* (New York: Arno Press, 1839).

15 Vanessa Northington Gamble, "Under the Shadow of Tuskegee: African Americans and Health Care," *American Journal of Public Health* 87, no. 11 (November 1997).

16 Fry, *Night Riders in Black Folk History*, 210.

17 *Nebraska State Journal*, October 22, 1893.

18 Frederick C. Waite, "Grave Robbing in New England," *Medical Library Association Bulletin* 33 (1945), 272–294.

19 *Janesville (WI) Gazette*, January 23, 1872.

20 *Spirit Lake Messenger*, April 9, 1886.

21 The idea of night doctors was so pervasive that on August 18, 1907, the *Washington Post* ran an urban legend–type story about the famed sculptor Augustus St. Gaudens. He approached a black man on the streets of Washington, D.C., and asked him to model for a statue of a soldier. The man thought St. Gaudens was a night doctor and ran away; the artist took off after him, and a policeman, thinking that St. Gaudens was chasing a thief, lit out after both. A cartoon depicts all three running down the street.

22 Mary E. Lyons, *Raw Head, Bloody Bones: African-American Tales of the Supernatural* (New York: Atheneum, 1991), 47–50.

23 *Spirit Lake Beacon*, April 9, 1886.

24 Fry, *Night Riders in Black Folk History*, 201. On p. 161 of Rev. Montague Summers's *History of Witchcraft and Demonology* (1926), he tells a similar story: "It was long thought by the ignorant country folk that the doctors of the hospital of Graz enjoyed the privilege of being allowed every year to exploit one human life for curative purposes. Some young man who repaired thither for toothache or any such slight ailment is seized, hung up by his feet, and tickled to death! Skilled chemists boil the body to a paste and utilize this as well as the fat and the charred bones in their drug store." Like the doctors at Graz, night doctors had designated times to find victims. Summers's source is Victor Fossel's *Volksmedicin und Medicinis Cher Aberglaube in Steiermark*, which was published in 1886; the year the story appeared in the *Spirit Lake Beacon*.

25 Fry, *Night Riders in Black Folk History*, 210–211.

26 Michael Newton, *The Encyclopedia of Serial Killers* (New York: Checkmark Books, 2000), 102.

27 BACM Research, *Atlanta Child Murders: Wayne Williams FBI Files*, dclxxxviii.

28 Ibid., dclxxxix.

29 "Atlanta Child Murders," CNN Live Event/Special, June 10, 2010. Transcript available at http://transcripts.cnn.com/TRANSCRIPTS/1006/10/se.01.html.

30 Ibid.

31 Bernard D. Headley, *The Atlanta Youth Murders and the Politics of Race* (Carbondale: Southern Illinois University Press, 1998), 126.

32 http://abj.matrix.msu.edu/videofull.php?id=29-DF-1E.

33 James Baldwin, *The Evidence of Things Not Seen* (New York: Holt, 1985), 87.

34 Gamble, "Under the Shadow of Tuskegee," 1773–1777.

35 *Valley Independent*, June 5, 1981.

36 Consider an unrelated incident of mass hysteria in Bristol, Virginia, in 2010. Amid rumors that a bloodthirsty vampire cult might ritualistically sacrifice their children to gain immortality, dozens of Wallace Middle School parents kept their kids home Friday. Washington County [Virginia] County School Superintendent Alan T. Lee said the panic grew from a wildly overblown story about an online "hit-list." It likely began with "a 'hate-list' posted anonymously on a website called VampireFreaks.com" that "reportedly included everything from Barack Obama to country music to this group of middle school girls." Concerned parents sent the information back and forth, and "Somewhere along the line 'hate list' became 'hit list,' and panic spread that a vampire cult infiltrated the Washington County public school." *Bristol (VA) Herald Courier,* December 24, 2012.

37 http://slic.njstatelib.org/new_jersey_information/digital_collections/unit_9_world_war_i_and_the_great_migration_1915_1920.

38 Among the few clues relating to the disappearance of the "Clinton Avenue Five" was a phone call made to one of their relatives from someone claiming that the five had been arrested. This was not true, but the call originated from Union Station in Washington, D.C., which was once notorious for night doctor activity.

39 *Daily Herald (Chicago, IL)*, October 31, 1980.

40 Fry, *Night Riders in Black Folk History*, 190–191.

41 *The (Frederick, MD) News*, November 2, 1995.

42 Scott Wood, *London Urban Legends* (Stroud, UK: History Press, 2013), 132.

43 Christopher Berry-Dee, *The Voices of the Serial Killers* (Berkeley, CA: Ulysses Press, 2011), 45.

44 Jaye Fletcher, *Deadly Thrills* (New York: Onyx Books, 1995), 54, 77.

45 Patricia A. Turner, *I Heard It Through the Grapevine* (Berkeley: University of California Press, 1993), 27.

46 W.E.B. DuBois Institute, *Black Imagination and the Middle Passage* (New York: Oxford University Press, 1999), 38.

47 Johannes Postma, *The Dutch in the Atlantic Slave Trade, 1600–1815* (Cambridge: Cambridge University Press, 2008), 165.

48 William Arens, *Man-Eating Myth*, 22, cited in Turner, *I Heard It Through the Grapevine*, 139.

The Blood Gospel

1 *Daily Boomerang (WY)*, January 27, 1890.

2 *Brooklyn (NY) Daily Eagle*, January 27, 1890.

3 Ibid.

4 Ibid.

5 Ibid.

6 Ibid.

7 Ibid.

8 *New York Times*, July 9, 1898.

9 *Galveston News*, May 21, 1883.

10 *Fresno (CA) Republican*, July 28, 1877.

11 *Stevens Point (WI) Daily Journal*, June 9, 1883.

12 *Daily Free Press (WI)*, September 14, 1875.

13 *Warren (PA) Ledger*, January 3, 1879.

14 *Bucks County (PA) Gazette*, May 8, 1890.

15 *Daily Free Press*, September 14, 1875.

16 Robert Withers, ed., *Controversies in Analytical Psychology* (New York: Brunner-Routledge, 2003), 64.

17 *Daily Free Press*, September 14, 1875; *Waterloo (IA) Courier*, May 31, 1876.

18 http://www.mirror.co.uk/news/weird-news/vampire-mum-of-two-i-drink-two-1943342.

19 *Stevens Point Daily Journal*, June 3, 1883; Judith Walzer Leavitt and Ronald Numbers, *Sickness and Health in America* (Madison: University of Wisconsin Press, 1997), 5. *Consumption* was used to describe any form of wasting illness. Tuberculosis is also closely

associated with vampirism in New England; see Michael E. Bell's book *Food for the Dead: On the Trail of New England's Vampires* (New York: Carroll & Graf, 2001).

20 "*Der Arme Heinrich von Hartmann von der Aue*" (Berlin, 1815), quoted in Hermann Leberecht Strack, *The Jew and Human Sacrifice* (London: Cope and Fenwick, 1909), 62.

21 Pliny the Elder, quoted in Owsei Temkin, *The Falling Sickness* (Baltimore: Johns Hopkins University Press, 2010).

22 Armando R. Favazza, *Bodies under Siege* (Baltimore: Johns Hopkins University Press, 2011), 6.

23 *Targum Pseudo-Jonathan*, quoted in Strack, *The Jew and Human Sacrifice*, 63.

24 Hermann Leberecht Strack, *The Jew and Human Sacrifice*, 63.

25 G. Daniel, *Histoire de France*, IX, 1755, quoted in Strack, *The Jew and Human Sacrifice*, 65.

26 Personal communication to the author from David W. Jackson, Director of Archives and Education at the Jackson County (Missouri) Historical Society, June 13, 2007.

27 James Hastings, ed., *Encyclopedia of Religion and Ethics*, vol. 2 (New York: Scribner, 1910), 715.

Afterword

1 *New York Times*, March 31, 1922.

2 *Washington Times*, June 17, 1906.

3 *Daily Milwaukee News*, March 11, 1866.

4 *New York Daily Tribune*, June 24, 1906.

5 *Monroe (MI) Commercial*, March 8, 1877; *Monroe (MI) Democrat*, August 21, 1884.

INDEX

Index

Index

INDEX

Index

Index

Index

Index

Index